MAKE FRIENDS WITH YOUR SHADE TREES

JERRY BAKER

Designed and Edited by Charles Cook

Simon and Schuster   New York

Special thanks to my friends Linda Gray
and Louise Riotte for their valuable assistance
in the preparation of this book.

We would like to thank the following individuals
and organizations for providing the photographs
which appear in this book:
Cook—18, 34, 62, 64; H. Armstrong Roberts—13;
Roche—71; Paris Trail—14, 15; Pennsylvania State
University—50; Wilkinson—4, 6, 8, 9, 12, 15, 17, 19,
20, 21, 24, 25, 29, 36, 37, 42, 43, 47, 54, 58, 70, 71.

Published by Simon and Schuster
Rockefeller Center, 630 Fifth Avenue
New York, New York 10020

SBN 671-21655-4 Paperback
Library of Congress Catalog Card Number: 73-8222
Designed by Charles Cook
Manufactured in the United States of America

1   2   3   4   5   6   7   8   9   10

Cover photo by Yard & Fruit

Contents

*"Mother was right! I did grow up
into a beautiful tree—I was afraid
I'd be an acorn forever."*

Shade Trees Are Cool

Have you ever spent a sultry summer afternoon sipping lemonade in the shade of a giant tree? Did you ever swing from a board or tire hung from the branches of a tree in your backyard? Or maybe you've sought relief from some of life's tensions walking among the trees in a city park. If you've done any of these things, you know what an important part trees play in our lives and our landscape.

Probably, though, you take shade trees for granted—unless you've just moved into a new house in the middle of a bare lot. I've never been able to understand why so many contractors feel compelled to chop down every tree in sight before they start building. Not long ago, I was driving through a newly completed suburb, and I didn't see a single tree larger than 6 inches in diameter. The houses were very attractive, but the people who move into them will have a lot of work to do before they turn them into homes. Of course, the first thing they'll do is seed their lawns. After that, they'll plant shade trees—or they should.

If these new homeowners are smart, they'll give a lot of thought to the trees they choose; they won't just dash down to the nearest discount garden center and grab the first—and the cheapest—tree they see. Trees are long-term investments, and if you choose and plant them wisely, they will add to the beauty and value of your home. They can complement the lines of your house, provide a background for flower beds, shade your outdoor living area, and screen out unpleasant views. And many trees are attractive enough to stand alone as specimen plants.

There are more than 2,000 species and varieties of deciduous trees that can be grown somewhere in the United States. Of course, all of these trees are not suitable for all climates and all purposes, but there's bound to be at least one tree perfectly suited to your particular needs. The problem is finding it. Believe it or not, that's a lot easier than finding a needle in a haystack.

Actually, choosing a shade tree is a lot like choosing a husband or wife. You meet a lot of people, and then suddenly you meet one that you know is just right for you. So you get married, and that's a choice meant to last a lifetime. When you choose a tree, you decide exactly what your needs are and what you can offer the tree to which you propose. Then you get to know a lot of trees by driving around your town, visiting nurseries and reading books. Finally you find a tree that you know is just right for you so you take it home, promise to care for it till death do you part, and live happily ever after.

A Question of Compatibility

The first thing you need to decide about a tree you meet is whether it will be happy at your home. Will it be able to adapt to the climate and soil conditions you have to offer? The nurseries in your area probably don't carry plants that won't adapt to the climate; but if you're ordering from a mail-order nursery you'll have to do some detective work to find out if the beauty you've decided on will thrive in your part of the country.

One of the best ways to find out what trees do best in your area is to take a leisurely drive through some of the older neighborhoods in your town. Notice which trees look strong and healthy. You might also pay attention to the size and shapes of trees so you'll know what your babies will look like when they grow up.

Your second consideration should be the tree's susceptibility to diseases and insect infestations. Elms, for example, are notoriously susceptible to Dutch elm disease. Avoid trees that you might have to coddle through a series of illnesses.

Next find out if the tree you're considering has any bad habits. Some are very messy.

They litter up their homes with twigs, seed pods or fruit. The silver maple, though very popular, has a careless habit of dropping its brittle twigs all over the lawn. Horse chestnuts scatter their nuts, which are inedible, over a wide area. Stay away from these and other litterbugs unless you can plant them in an out-of-the-way location or don't mind doing a lot of raking.

A Growing Concern

Last, but certainly not least, is the question of size. Just how big is that little whip you're buying going to get? A sugar maple may reach a soaring 80 feet. If you live in a two-story house, a sugar maple would look fine beside it, but it would overpower a low ranch-style home on a small lot. Try to choose trees that will be in proportion to your house and lot when they reach maturity.

Size also dictates the spacing of trees. You need to know how close you can plant a tree to your house, your driveway, the street or other trees. Find out how far the branches will spread. Don't just guess or you may find yourself being crowded out of your own yard in a few years. Also remember to keep trees as far away from your flower beds as possible to prevent the roots from creeping in and robbing your flowers of moisture and nutrients.

A lady I know bought four 3-foot tall red oaks. She had read that these trees would eventually reach a height of 75 feet and spread as far as 50 feet, but when she looked at those tiny trees, she just couldn't believe it. So she planted the trees in a line, 20 feet away from each other and 20 feet away from the side of her house. The trees looked fine for the first 2 or 3 years, but then they began to crowd each other and the house. The trees are now rubbing noses with one another and smacking the lady's bedroom window with their branches. Pretty soon she's going to be faced with the task of removing most if not all of these trees.

As you can see from the photo on the opposite page, tall, massive shade trees tend to overpower modern ranch-style homes.

"All right, Fred, if you buy this tree instead of a new refrigerator, I'm going home to Mother!"

Think Positive!

Now that we've discussed the reasons for not buying certain trees, let's move to a brighter subject—the reasons to buy certain trees.

The first consideration in choosing a shade tree is, obviously, shade. All trees do produce shade, but all shade is not alike. Chances are when you think of shade trees, you think of tall spreading maples and oaks. And these old favorites are excellent choices if you want a wide area of deep shade and if you have plenty of room. Maples and oaks, as well as tulip trees, lindens, elms, poplars and other trees which often exceed 50 feet in height, should be planted at least 30 feet away from your house, the street and other trees. If you do plant these giants too near your house, you'll spend more time cleaning leaves out of the gutter than sitting in the shade.

If you don't have room for one of the 50-footers in your yard, you can still have all the shade you want. The yellowwood, for instance, provides a wide area of dense, cool shade, but grows only 35 to 50 feet tall. If you need an even smaller tree, you might consider some of the flowering trees, many of which never exceed 30 feet in height. Fruit trees can double as shade trees, too.

Flowering trees and fruit trees do not cast such dense shade as some of their big brothers, but this is sometimes an advantage. Maples, oaks, yellowwoods and other tall trees with thick foliage cast shade so deep that grass doesn't grow well beneath them. And unless you live in an area with a sizzling summer climate, you would probably prefer lighter shade and thicker grass. If so, you might also consider some of the fine foliaged trees, such as Jerusalem thorns, silk trees and thornless honey locusts. The light, filtered shade these trees cast allows you to grow grass and even shade-loving flowers beneath their branches.

You've probably seen locusts growing wild, and you may have noticed that they have some very bad habits—a thorny disposition and a slovenly habit of littering the ground with their seed pods. Let me reassure you that the thornless honey locust is much more well bred than his cousins. Not only does it have no thorns and no seed pods, its leaves are so fine and feathery that you probably won't even have to rake them up when they fall. They will disappear into the grass and decay, saving you work and enriching the soil as well.

The Lollipop Tree

When I was a child, I drew trees and lollipops the same way. Both had a round circle on top of a stick or trunk. The only difference was that lollipops were red and trees were green. As I grew older, I discovered that no tree is really shaped like a lollipop. At that point in my life, I decided I could never win fame and fortune as an artist.

I have since learned that trees grow in several basic shapes—vase-shaped, broad and spreading, oval, pyramidal, weeping and irregularly shaped. There are also variations of these basic forms such as rounded, fan-shaped, multiple-stemmed and horizontally-branched. Of course, the shape of a tree is also affected by the location in which it grows. Trees growing in groups or in woodlands have to compete for sunlight, so they tend to grow taller and thinner than they would if grown in the open. Planted alone in full sun, a tree will assume an even, natural shape.

You need to know what shape a tree will be at maturity before you buy it so you can tell if it will fulfill your landscaping needs. Trees with a horizontal branch pattern, for example, will soften tall vertical lines. A tree with high arching branches, such as the Japanese pagoda tree, makes a better shade

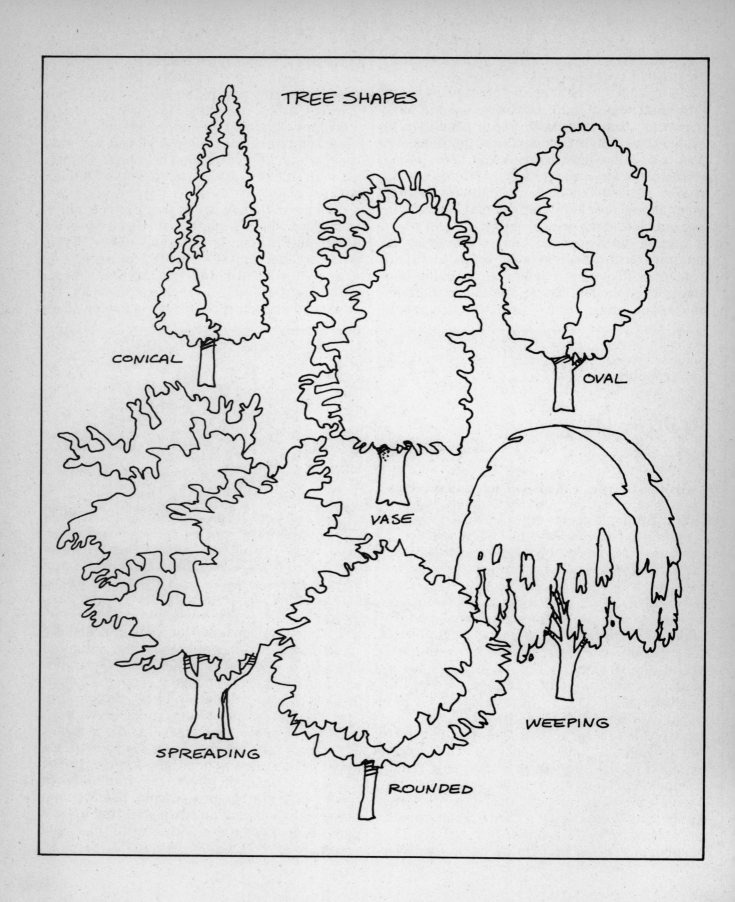

TREE SHAPES

CONICAL

VASE

OVAL

SPREADING

ROUNDED

WEEPING

tree than one with low branches and a conical top, such as the pin oak.

Shape also determines the amount of lawn space a tree will take up. Weeping willows are very beautiful, but they take up a tremendous amount of space for the shade they cast. Red oaks, on the other hand, produce a wide area of deep shade but take up very little lawn space. They are, however, very tall and spreading. Sugar maples are tall too, but their branches are more upright than spreading, so they can be planted closer to buildings and other trees.

As I said before, maples, oaks and other giants tend to overpower smaller suburban homes and yards. In these situations, a group of smaller trees might be better than one monstrous shade tree. Slender trees, such as goldenrain or persimmon, are good choices for grouping.

Strength in Numbers

Groups of trees can also be used as screens. They give more privacy than shrub hedges, and, if properly located, they can produce a wide area of shade. For an effective screen, stay away from high-branched trees such as tulip trees and sycamores; instead choose trees with low, spreading branches, such as the pin oak or magnolia. For a more formal screen, plant tall, columnar trees close together. The Lombardy poplar is probably the most popular tree for this purpose, but I prefer the pyramidal hornbeam. Lombardy poplars grow extremely fast and reach a height of 30 to 50 feet very rapidly, but are very short-lived. These poplars are also susceptible to a canker disease which attacks the upper trunk and branches and ruins the symmetry of the tree. The pyramidal hornbeam seldom exceeds 30 feet in height, which makes it suitable for the smallest yards, and its profile is much less ragged than that of the Lombardy poplar. The hornbeam's neat branching habit, smooth blue-gray bark and reddish brown leaf buds give it an elegant appearance even in winter. The only problem with this dapper gentleman is that once he settles down and becomes established, he doesn't like to be disturbed, so buy the smallest plants you can find.

With a little imagination, you can make a small yard seem larger by placing groups of trees so that they divide the yard into several small areas. For this purpose, you don't want trees that will completely block your vision. Instead, choose relatively small trees with multiple trunks, such as redbuds, birches, and saucer magnolias. You'll be able to see through these trees, but they will create the illusion of dividing your yard into outdoor rooms. You might, for example, use a clump of trees to divide off an outdoor eating area, a play area or maybe a lounging-in-the-shade area.

Closing Up Those Wide, Open Spaces

If you've just moved into a brand new house, you're probably already visualizing the way you want it to look. You've seen a chair that would be perfect in the living room, curtains that match the paint in the kitchen and a dozen other things that would help you turn your house into a home. And then there's the yard. Not a tree in sight. The obvious solution to this problem is to go right out and buy everything you need, including a bag of grass seed, some flower seeds and the largest trees you can find. But after you've made the downpayment on your house, paid the movers, made deposits at the electric company and the waterworks and accumulated a long list of miscellaneous expenses, you probably can't afford to even think of landscaping your yard—at least not for a while.

When your budget recovers a little, the first things you'll want to do are seed the lawn and plant trees. After all, you do want to make a good impression on your new neighbors as soon as possible. When you go shopping for trees, you'll probably find that a substantial tree, one 20 to 25 feet tall, for instance, will cost about as much as a new refrigerator. If you're planning to stay in your new home for a long time, a large tree might be a good investment—if you can afford it. If you can't or if you'll be moving on in a few years, you probably don't want to make such a large expenditure. So what you need are some fast-growing trees.

Ten-Year Titans

Unfortunately, there are no trees that will grow as fast as Jack's legendary beanstalk, but there are trees which will grow to a respectable size in 10 years. Silver maples and London plane trees will grow from a height of 8 to 10 feet at planting time to about 35 feet in 10 years. Eight- to ten-feet-tall

Try a speedy silk tree.

horse chestnuts, European hackberries, thornless honey locusts and moraine ashes will reach a height of 20 to 25 feet in 10 years. Silk trees, Jerusalem thorns, mulberries, Russian olives and Kaki persimmons will grow from a height of 6 feet at planting time to 20 feet or more in 5 years. There are, of course, many other fast-growing treees to choose from.

Fast-growing trees are usually cheaper than their slow-growing cousins because nurseries can sell them at a younger age. They do have disadvantages, though. Fast-growing trees tend to be brittle and are, therefore, subject to breakage. Plant them only if you don't mind their sloppy habit of dropping broken twigs and branches on your lawn. Many of them also have shallow, spreading root systems which can interfere with sewers, sidewalks and flower beds.

I suggest that you plant some fast-growing, long-lived trees as well. Let the eager beavers provide shade and beauty until the slower trees grow large enough to add their dignity to the landscape. If the fast-growing trees become unsightly, as they get older, you can remove them.

Fruit Trees

Many trees produce much more than shade—namely, flowers, fruits or nuts. Some of the fruits and nuts have only ornamental value, but others are not just edible—they're delicious! Pecans, walnuts, Chinese chestnuts, mulberries, persimmons, figs, pears and oranges are among the fruits and nuts you could pick from the shade trees in your back yard. I think everyone should have at least one fruit or nut tree in his yard. I have several fruit trees in my yard, and I can tell you there are few pleasures in life greater than going out on a fine summer morning to pick a basket of peaches from my own trees. And children love fruit trees, as you'll remember if you ever sat high in the branches of an apple tree and ate all you could hold.

Fruit and nut trees come in all shapes and sizes. Many of the dwarf fruit trees stand less than 10 feet tall at maturity; their standard-size brothers seldom exceed 25 feet in height. The small size of these trees makes

pruning and harvesting convenient, but if you need a taller, slimmer, tree, you might prefer a black mulberry, which grows to about 30 feet, or a native persimmon, which grows from 35 to 50 feet tall with a spread of 20 to 30 feet. Unripe persimmons are mouth-puckeringly sour, but when ripe they are sweet and delicious. Nut trees are generally larger than fruit trees. Walnut trees grow about 50 feet tall, and pecans may reach a height of 100 feet with a spread of 40 to 75 feet.

When you're shopping for fruit or nut trees, make sure you choose types which will bear in your area. An apple tree would grow in Florida, but it would never bear fruit in that frost-free climate. An orange tree, on the other hand, would not survive its first winter in Vermont. In other words, a tree that is hardy in your area may not bear fruit, but if a tree isn't hardy it certainly won't bear fruit. To find out which fruit and nut trees will do well where you live, call your county agent or nurseryman. Either man should also be able to tell you what varieties are best and whether you need to buy two trees of opposite sex to insure pollination and fruiting.

There are, of course, trees which flower but bear inedible or insignificant fruit or nuts. The dogwoods, for instance, are beautiful when in flower, but their red, berry-like fruits are small and unremarkable. Because trees bear their fruits high above eye level, those bearing small fruits are less valuable ornamentally than many of the fruiting shrubs. This does not mean that these trees are not valuable for other reasons. Flowering cherries, peaches and plums are truly spectacular when they're in bloom, but their fruits are miniature versions of that produced by their cousins in the orchard. Some of these trees bear no fruit at all. Hybridizers have bred these trees for blossoms rather than fruit, and I think Mother Nature thanks them for improving on her efforts.

A Full Season of Flowers

If you're planting trees that bear large, soft fruits, keep them away from your patio, sidewalk and clothesline. Most are very generous with their fruit—so generous that they drop some fruit on the ground. If you want blossoms but can do without bruised fruit underfoot, plant flowering trees that

Mulberries, apples, walnuts and plums are only part of the harvest you can reap from the shade trees in your own back yard.

bear no fruit in heavily trafficked areas.

Not all flowering trees bloom in the spring, though many of the most popular ones do. If you choose carefully, you can have trees in flower at various times throughout spring, summer and fall. You're probably already familiar with most of the spring-flowering trees, but have you ever met the waterer laburnum? In mid-spring it bears masses of bright yellow blossoms in pendulous clusters which may be as long as 20 inches. The flower clusters of the Scotch laburnum are a little

smaller, but it has a weeping branch pattern which makes the blossoms even more striking. A little later, in early summer, the goldenrain tree bursts into blooms. It, too, bears long clusters of yellow flowers, but they are borne in an erect position. Neither of these golden beauties exceeds 25 feet in height, so either could be included in even the smallest landscape plan.

There are many other summer-flowering trees. If you'd like a cooling splash of white in your summer landscape, you might choose a yellowwood, a black locust, a fringe tree, a silver linden or a sorrel tree. All these trees are also fragrant. Try planting one of these white-flowered, fragrant trees near your porch or patio. Try to place the tree so the fragrance will drift across the patio on the wind. For an even more dramatic effect, arrange an outdoor light so that the tree is softly illuminated; don't aim a glaring spotlight at it. When the tree is in full bloom, invite some friends over for a late supper and serve it outdoors. Half the fun of gardening is sharing your success with your family and friends.

Fall Colors

For fall blossoms, plant a Japanese pagoda tree or a franklinia. The pagoda tree bears 10- to 15-inch-long clusters of tiny, white blossoms in late summer or early autumn. It also makes an excellent shade tree because of its broad, spreading growth habit. The franklinia is not as good a shade tree as the pagoda tree, but its flowering habit alone makes it worthwhile. Mother Nature wasn't satisfied with producing flowers in spring and summer and brilliant foliage in the fall, so she put the two together in the franklinia. It bears 3-inch, fragrant white flowers just as its leaves are turning red or orange. Unfortunately, neither the franklinia nor the Japanese pagoda tree blossoms until it is 7 to 10 years old. Be patient. Both of the autumn jewels are worth the wait.

Fancy Foliage

Basic green is always good, but even Mother Nature occasionally wants a change of pace. In the fall, she and Jack Frost get together and paint the forest red—and yellow and orange. And she's tinted the leaves of some trees so they'll be bright and gay in the spring and summer when Jack Frost isn't around.

If you sometimes get a little tired of green, maybe you should get acquainted with some of Mother Nature's fancy-foliaged favorites. The gray-green Russian olive, the yellow leaf box elder, the red bloodleaf Japanese maple, the bronze spiderleaf Japanese maple, and the purple beech are among the trees you can choose from. All of these retain their distinctive foliage colors throughout the growing season. I wouldn't recommend planting a lot of trees with bright-colored foliage unless you want your yard to look like a patchwork quilt. Actually, trees with colored foliage look best used as an accent, either standing alone or in a group of green-leaved trees.

A Fall Fling with Jack Frost

If the trees take on brilliant fall colors where you live you're very fortunate. Aside from areas in the United States and Canada, brilliant autumn coloration occurs only in a small area in South America, a small section of southwestern Europe and a fairly large area in eastern Asia. In North America, autumn coloration occurs in an area extending from the Gulf of St. Lawrence to Florida and westward to the Great Plains. Farther west, fall colors appear at high altitudes. The most brilliant colors are found in southeastern Canada and in the northeastern United States.

In autumn, this rustic corner will be even more charming than it is in summer.

A CATALOG OF AUTUMN COLOR

Red

Vine maple (red to orange)
Amur maple
Manchurian maple
Japanese maple
Swamp maple
Franklinia (orange to red)
Sweet gum
Sargent cherry
Sassafras
Folger mountain ash
Stewartia
Alleghany serviceberry (yellow to red)
American hornbeam (orange to red)
Flowering dogwood
American smoke tree
Lavalle hawthorn (bronze-red)
Dawson crab apple
Red oak
Scarlet oak
Pin oak
Black oak

Yellow

Bigleaf maple
Norway maple
Ohio buckeye
Redbuds
Apple serviceberry
American yellowwood
White ash
Star magnolia
Shingle oak (russet)
Pawpaw
Birches
Hickories
Pecan
Chinese chestnut
Fringe tree
Beeches
Gingko
Golden larch
Korean mountain ash (orange to yellow)

Some Subtle Surprises

When most people think of a winter landscape, they visualize a Christmas-card scene full of snow-covered evergreens. And evergreens do play an important part in both winter and summer landscapes. Their fresh green color is a welcome relief from the browns, grays and white that dominate Mother Nature's winter wardrobe. But we wouldn't overlook the subtle beauties that deciduous trees display in winter.

In spring, summer and fall, the foliage hides or overshadows many of a tree's other features, such as its branch pattern, bark texture and overall density. Of course, these features don't have as much impact on the landscape as the foliage, but they shouldn't be ignored.

You should do your landscaping so that there are points of interest in every season. A burst of spring color is fine, but what about the rest of the year? Especially the winter. You're not going to hibernate with the bears. You probably won't be spending as much time in your yard as you did during the warmer months of the year, but unless you're going to draw the curtains and watch television all winter, you will be looking out your windows from time to time. So when you're doing your landscaping, give some thought to the winter view you're creating.

Does one of your windows look out on a blank wall or fence? You could plant evergreens in front of it, but they would look the same all year long. Some deciduous trees cast interesting shadow patterns when their branches are bare. Some of these are:

Staghorn sumac	Fringe tree
Redbud	Silk tree
Flowering dogwood	Black walnut
Red oak	Gingko
Yellowwood	Shagbark hickory
Goldenrain tree	Catalpa

An interesting branching pattern contributes to a tree's beauty in winter and summer alike.

Bare Is Beautiful!

Also consider the pattern the branches and twigs will make against the sky. Landscape architects call this texture. Some trees, such as the sweet gum, have a coarse texture. Their stout branches and twigs create a dramatic effect when these trees are planted alone on the lawn, against a rustic wood background or in front of a tall wall or building. Too many coarse-textured trees, however, lose their individual impact and become monotonous. It's best to use only a few with about twice as many fine-textured trees, such as Russian olive, beech, hornbeam and locust. The delicate twigs and branches of these trees etch a fine tracery against the sky.

The many different colors and textures of bark create subtle but beautiful contrasts in the landscape.

Be a Bark Shark

The bark of deciduous trees deserves much more attention than it receives. I think the trees resent this. They're proud of their complexions and want them to be noticed. The next time you're in a park or forest, take notice of all the different kinds of bark there are. Bark colors vary from the white of beeches to the deep black of the black walnut. The sargent cherry and other cherries have lustrous red bark. The Chinese paper birch, which is not as popular as it should be in this country, has bright orange bark. If you're looking for something really different, this bright-barked birch is for you.

The texture of bark is as important as its color. The smooth, light gray bark of beeches is distinctive in both winter and summer. You've probably noticed the beautiful flaking bark of birches and sycamores, but you may not know that other trees have this same delightful habit. The stewartias, the lacebark maple and the shagbark hickory are among the best of these.

If you get to know your trees, you can have far more than shade. Flowers, fruit, nuts, autumn color and winter beauty are the fringe benefits of choosing trees wisely.

Don't be fooled by the gingko's delicate fan-shaped leaves; it's tough enough to survive the air pollution in our over-crowded cities.

Problem Children

Almost every homeowner has at least one gardening problem to overcome. Maybe you live in a city where pollution makes life miserable for trees and people alike. Or maybe you have a low, wet spot that frogs love but you hate. Trees can solve all these problems and more.

If you need a tree that can make it as a city slicker, choose one of the following:

Hedge maple
Box elder
Norway maple
Sycamore maple
Ohio buckeye
Baumann horse chestnut
Tree of heaven
Southern magnolia
Saucer magnolia
Japanese pagoda tree

Silk tree
Catalpa
Hackberry
Russian olive
White ash
Gingko
Goldenrain tree
Crab apple
White poplar
Red oak

Some trees don't even mind wet feet. If you have a wet spot try a swamp maple, an elder, a sweet bay or a willow. If dry or poor soil is your problem, the box elder, the silk tree, the bauhinias, the gray birch and the European hackberry are all willing to come to your rescue.

The Norway maple, the velvet ash, the Calfornia live oak, and the holly oak are among the trees suitable for inclusion in seaside gardens. Many others will tolerate sandy soil, and some will even stand up to salt spray.

Don't be fooled by the gingko's delicate fan-shaped leaves; it's tough enough to survive the air pollution in our over-crowded cities.

The Plan

I can't emphasize too strongly the need for planning before planting trees. Trees live for many years, so you're going to have to live with your initial decisions for a long time. Nothing makes more impact on a landscape than trees. If you plant one in the wrong place, it will stand as a monument to your carelessness for years.

Go out in your yard and look around. Are there any dead or dying trees? Or any trees that detract from the landscape? If so, remove them. I don't have to tell you that removing a tree is no easy task, so consider your decision carefully.

Where should you plant new trees? If you want them to shade the house, place them on the south and west sides for maximum cooling. If you want to shade a particular outdoor area, hold a broom or fishing pole above your head and stand between the sun and the area you want to shade. Your neighbors may think you're a little strange, but pay no attention. Move around until the shade of the pole falls in the right place, then stop and mark the spot. (If the tree will be taller than the pole, you can estimate the length of the tree's shadow as best you can.) Now drive a stake in that spot and mark the spread of the mature tree around it. Is it too close to the house or other trees? If so, move the stake back. Leave the stake in place for a few days and look at the shadow it casts at various times of the day. The area should at least be shaded during the time of day when it is most frequently used.

It's in the Bag!

Now it's time to make a paper-bag plan. Tear open and flatten a large grocery bag. You can buy a large sheet of paper if you want, but grocery bags have the advantage of being free. Make a scale drawing of your yard, including your house, garage, trees, hedges, flower beds and sidewalks. Mark north and south with large letters. Indicate any problem areas, such as wet spots. Also mark the location of water or sewer lines and overhead utility wires. Now, using another sheet of paper, cut out circles representing the mature spread of trees you may buy. Label each one. Move them around on your paper-bag plan until you've decided where each should be planted. Experimenting on paper is a lot easier than playing musical chairs with your trees after they've been planted, so keep working until you have exactly what you want.

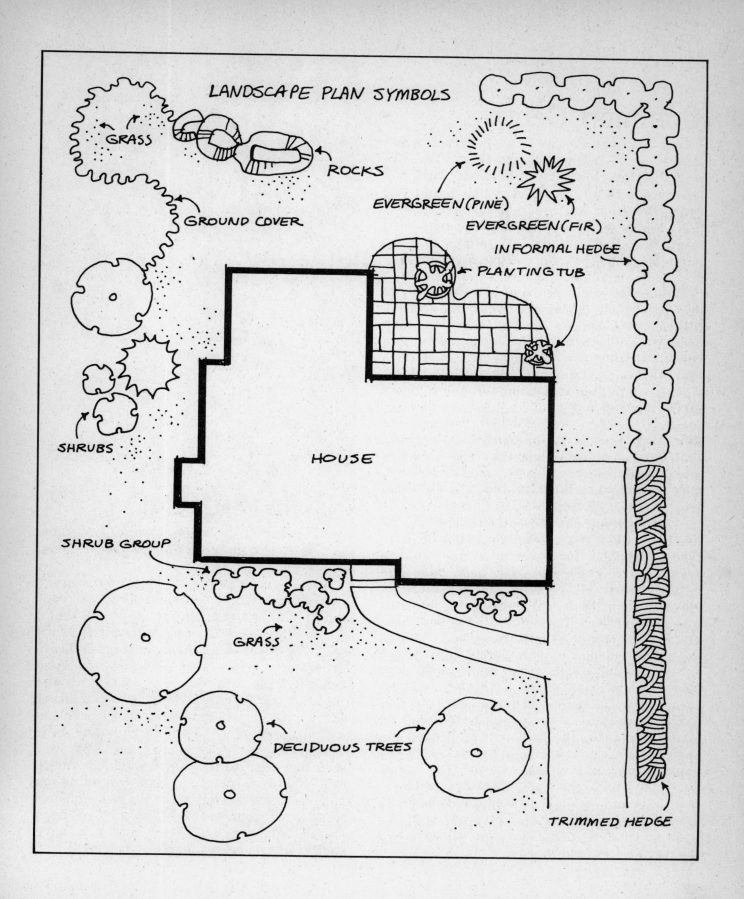

LANDSCAPE PLAN SYMBOLS

GRASS

ROCKS

GROUND COVER

EVERGREEN (PINE)

EVERGREEN (FIR)

INFORMAL HEDGE

PLANTING TUB

SHRUBS

HOUSE

SHRUB GROUP

GRASS

DECIDUOUS TREES

TRIMMED HEDGE

Common Cents

Now you know what trees you want and where you're going to plant them. You can probably imagine just what your yard will look like with all the trees in place, and you probably can't wait to get started. And I don't blame you. Landscaping your own yard is exciting. But too much excitement and not enough common sense can cost you money and cause a lot of disappointment.

When you decide to buy a new car, you don't go to one dealer and write out a check for the first car he shows you. You shop around, looking for just the car you want and the best price. In other words, you're a careful shopper. And you should be at least this careful when you shop for trees. After all, a tree will last a lot longer than any car you buy.

You can purchase trees at a local nursery or from a mail-order nursery. The only disadvantage of buying from a mail-order nursery is that you will be limited to fairly small trees. Generally, 5- to 6-feet tall trees are the largest that can conveniently be shipped by mail. However, if you want a number of small trees, perhaps for a windbreak, then a mail-order nursery is your best bet. The smaller trees will probably be considerably cheaper than the larger ones that your local nursery carries. Remember, however, that all cheap trees aren't bargains. You've probably opened your mailbox and found bright-colored catalogs that show trees with blossoms the size of dinner plates. And the copy promises that they'll shoot up so fast you'll think they're jet propelled. Best of all they're unbelievably cheap. Take if from me the low price is all you should believe. If you order some of these "bargains," your mailman will bring you a tiny box of poorly packaged anemic plants. If you can coax a few of them into growing, don't expect them to look anything like the beautiful trees in the catalog.

Horse Sense

Everybody knows you pick a good horse by looking at its teeth. And you pick a good watermelon by thumping it. But how do you pick a good tree?

First you need to know something about the way trees are sold. They come in three forms—bare-rooted, in containers, and balled and burlapped. Bare-root trees are the easiest to ship, but they must be handled with great care to prevent the roots from drying out. Trees in containers can be transplanted along with the soil in which they have been growing so there's no risk that the roots will dry out. The average container tree is rather small—about 3 or 4 feet high. If trees grown in standard 1-gallon cans are much larger than this, don't buy them. Their roots are badly crowded. Large trees, even full-grown shade trees, are sold balled and burlapped. If you do buy a large, balled and burlapped tree, you'll probably have to have the nurseryman plant it for you as even a relatively small ball of soil is very heavy.

When buying balled and burlapped trees, feel the ball of soil. If it is soft instead of hard and tightly packed, don't buy that tree. Its roots may be broken and there are certainly air pockets around them which will cause drying out. Also reject any tree whose trunk is loose in the ball of soil.

Examine the roots of container trees. They should fill the container. Ask the nurseryman to tilt the can and partially remove the root ball. If this is not possible, turn the can on its side and look at the drainage holes. If you can see the roots, you can be confident that the root system is well developed.

Look for broken branches and injured bark. Both are symptoms of poor handling and may admit disease. Also avoid any trees with wilted leaves as this means they have not been adequately watered. The leaves should also be a healthy, bright green color, not yellowish or pale.

"You're supposed to plant me promptly—but not this promptly!"

Wanted Dead or Alive

Even if you do pick out the best tree at the nursery, you can lose it on the ride home if you're not careful. I've seen people throw beautiful young trees into the back seat with their heads sticking out the windows. Those helpless trees didn't have a chance. The soil was undoubtedly jarred away from the roots, and the branches would certainly dry out on the ride home.

When you're acting as a tree chauffeur, be very gentle. If the tree is too large to fit comfortably in your car, have it delivered. Your nurseryman undoubtedly has trucks and any other equipment necessary to transport trees properly.

If you're buying trees that aren't yet leafed out, look at the buds to make sure the tree is still alive. If you can't tell, break a twig or small branch. If it snaps off very easily and the center is dried out rather than pithy, the tree is dead or dying. Not long ago, I visited a discount nursery center that was offering young shade trees at a very low price. I soon realized that the people buying those trees were going to be very disappointed. Most of the trees were already dead, but the unsuspecting customers obviously didn't realize this. If they had just taken the time to examine the trees closely, they would have saved themselves money, wasted effort and disappointment.

Transplanting

If you live in the country or have friends who do, you may not have to buy trees at all. You can transplant young trees from the forest into your front yard. This does not mean, however, that you can go out into the forest, carelessly dig up a tree, take it home with you and seriously expect it to do well. Being snatched up out of the cool, quiet woodland you love is a traumatic experience for a young tree, so you must help it adjust itself to a major change in lifestyle.

First, find a healthy, well-shaped tree. Trees taller than 6 or 8 feet may have difficulty adjusting to the shock of transplanting. Six months to a year before you want to move the tree to your yard, you must prune the roots. (Spring is the best time for this.) To do so, dig a trench as deep and as wide as your spade around the tree. For an 8 foot tree, the circle should have a radius of 8 to 10 inches. Fill the trench with a mixture of soil and peat moss and prune back the top branches by about a third to compensate for injury to the roots. Now leave the tree alone for about 6 months, during which time roots will form in the trench.

When you go back to dig up the tree, take along a sharp spade, a 4-foot-square piece of burlap and some sturdy cord. Dig a trench outside the first one and dig under the tree to free the soil ball and roots. Now roll up the burlap halfway. Carefully tilt the root ball so you can slip the rolled burlap under it. The unrolled half should extend up the side of the hole. Tilt the soil ball the other way and unroll the burlap. Loop two pieces of cord and roll them up in adjacent corners of the burlap. Roll up straight pieces in the 2 remaining corners. Now knot each cord and bring the corners together on top of the soil ball, pulling the straight cords through the

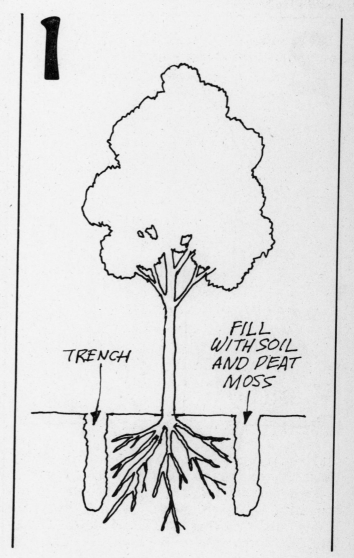

1

TRENCH

FILL WITH SOIL AND PEAT MOSS

looped ones. Tie the cords tightly and, if necessary, tie longer pieces around the soil ball both vertically and horizontally.

After you've planted the tree, be sure to wrap the trunk to protect it from sunscald. Trees grown in the shade of a forest are much more susceptible to sunscald than nursery-grown trees.

Admittedly, transplanting trees from the forest is a lot more difficult than buying them at a nursery, but occasionally you may fall in love with a lovely little tree you meet on a walk in the woods. If you want to share your home with her, take the time to move her correctly. I promise you'll both live happily ever after.

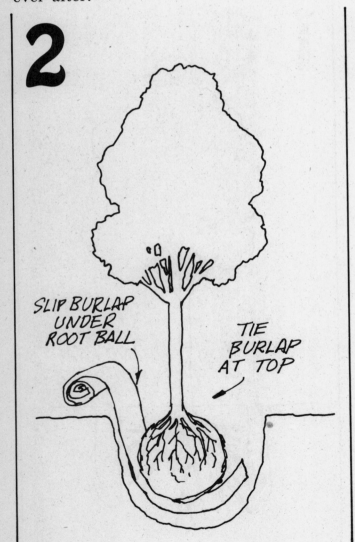

2

SLIP BURLAP UNDER ROOT BALL

TIE BURLAP AT TOP

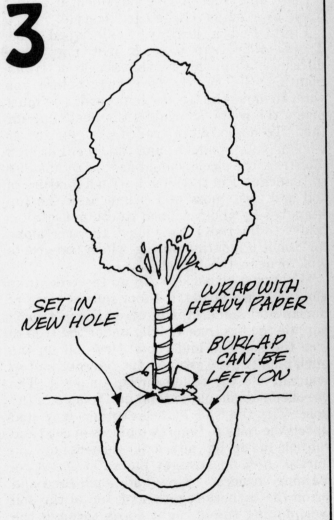

3

SET IN NEW HOLE

WRAP WITH HEAVY PAPER

BURLAP CAN BE LEFT ON

Timely Advice

The time to plant balled-and-burlapped and container trees is whenever you can get a spade into the ground. Bare-rooted trees should only be planted when they're dormant.

Even though trees can be planted at other times, I prefer planting in either spring or fall. Trees planted in the spring have several months to get established before winter sets in. Fall is a very pleasant time to plant because the soil is usually soft and moist, making digging easier, and the weather is cool and confortable. The roots will have enough time to make some progress before winter, and this root system will give fall-planted trees a head start over those planted the following spring.

Once you've bought a tree, it's up to you to make it happy in its new home. After all, it's not going to be a temporary guest; it's going to become a permanent member of your family. What's the first thing a couple does when they have a new baby? They give it a name, of course. They don't want to go on calling their beautiful, bouncing baby "he" or "she" forever. And you don't want to go on calling your tree "it" forever. Give it a name of its own and use it whenever you're scolding it or congratulating it on its progress.

Don't Treat Your Soil like Dirt

You think of soil as just dirt, but your tree doesn't. The soil is its home, and if it doesn't feel comfortable in the soil you provide, it will never be happy. So you need to find out if the soil where you're going to plant your tree is suitable. If it's not, you'll have to do something to make it suitable.

Most trees do best in a slightly acid soil, with a pH between 6 and 7. The only way to determine the acidity of your soil is with a

Balled-and-burlapped trees can be planted at any time during the year.

soil test. You can send a soil sample to your local agricultural extension service for testing or you can do the testing yourself with one of the kits available at most garden centers. Be sure to take samples from several locations in your yard and label them as the acidity may vary from place to place.

If the result of the test shows that the pH of the soil is unsuitable for the tree you want to grow, you can raise the pH (making the soil more alkaline) by adding limestone or lower it (making the soil more acid) by adding ground sulfur. To effectively change the soil acidity, you'll have to dig the limestone or sulfur into the soil to a depth of 18 inches or more. Spread the limestone or sulfur over a wide area to accommodate the tree's spreading roots. To make sure the pH is staying within a suitable range, test the soil every 3 or 4 years. You may have to add more limestone or sulfur from time to time.

Since changing the acidity of your soil is no easy task, you would be wise to choose trees that will be happy in your soil as it is. I always avoid finicky trees that I'll have to pamper for years, and so should you. You may not mind the extra care they demand at first, but eventually you'll start to resent them—and they'll know it.

Your soil may not be perfect—or even very good. It may be too clayey or too sandy. Clayey soils are heavy and tend to become waterlogged. Trees can literally drown in clayey soils. Sandy soils, on the other hand, are often too dry because they drain so quickly. Trees planted in sandy soils may die of thirst. Fortunately, one procedure will remedy both of these problems. The addition of liberal amounts of organic matter will lighten clay soils and will improve the water-holding capacity of sandy soils. For trees, you will have to work organic material into the soil over a wide area and to a depth of at least 18 inches.

If you have severe drainage problems caused, for example, by a layer of rock beneath the topsoil, you may have to install an underground drainage system. You can lay drainage pipes yourself, but since this is a

"Believe me, living in a sand castle is a draining experience."

very difficult task, you'll probably prefer to have it done by professionals. This will probably be an expensive undertaking, but it will permanently improve the condition of your soil.

Not all drainage problems are this severe. You may, for example, find a layer of impermeable, packed soil, called hardpan, at the bottom of the planting hole. To solve this problem, you must break through the hardpan to the looser soil beneath. Using a post-hole digger, dig a 6- to 8-inch-wide hole through the hardpan and fill the hole with coarse gravel. Water will drain out the hole, and your tree won't have a chronic case of wet feet.

Planting

The best advice I can give you on planting trees is to dig a $10 hole for a $5 tree. Nothing is worse for a young tree that's just trying to get established than having its tender roots shoved into a tight-fitting hole. If you've ever worn a pair of shoes that were too small, you know just how that tree feels. The situation will get worse when the tree starts to grow. The roots, which may already be injured, will have a hard time prying their way into the packed, hard soil around the planting hole. Eventually, the tree may just give up and die.

To prevent such a tragedy, when you dig your planting hole, make sure that the tree's roots will have plenty of room to grow in. As a general rule, the planting hole should be twice the diameter of the rootball and 1½ times as deep as the rootball is tall. Once the hole is dug, spread a layer of peat moss or leafmold in the bottom. Pack the organic

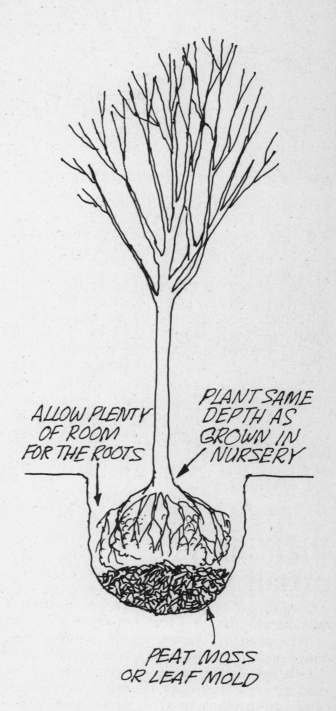

ALLOW PLENTY OF ROOM FOR THE ROOTS

PLANT SAME DEPTH AS GROWN IN NURSERY

PEAT MOSS OR LEAF MOLD

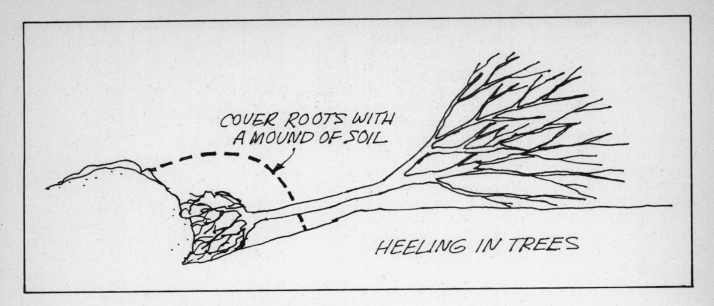

COVER ROOTS WITH A MOUND OF SOIL

HEELING IN TREES

material down firmly with your feet. Set the tree in the hole and check to see if it's sitting at the same depth as it was at the nursery. If it's not, adjust the depth of the layer of organic material.

A lot of container-grown trees lose their lives during clumsy attempts to remove them from their cans. Do not under any circumstances grasp the trunk of the tree and try to tug the rootball out of the can. If you're going to plant your tree soon after buying it, ask the nurseryman to cut the can and tie it to prevent its coming apart on the ride home. You can, of course, cut the container at planting time with a pair of tin snips. Pull the two halves of the cut container apart and carefully lift out the tree, grasping the ball of soil, not the trunk.

Planting Is a Ball

You do not have to remove burlap from a balled-and-burlapped tree before planting as it will soon decompose. It is a good idea, however, to loosen the burlap around the trunk and make sure there is no other material, such as canvas, inside the burlap.

If you're planting a bare-root tree, make sure the roots do not dry out. If you cannot plant it very soon after you receive it, heel it in a shallow trench and keep the soil moist. On the day of planting, take the tree out of the trench or remove the packing material and immediately plunge the roots into a pail of water. If the roots won't fit into a pail, wrap them in wet burlap or cover them with a heap of wet straw. Remember, if the roots ever become completely dry, the tree will die.

When planting balled-and-burlapped or container-grown trees, set the tree in the hole, making sure the soil ball is centered and the trunk is straight. Fill the hole three-quarters full of peat moss and soil, then firm it down with your feet. Now fill the hole with water, and when it has soaked in, finish filling the hole with soil and peat moss and tamp it down.

I always make a shallow, saucer-shaped basin around a newly planted tree to allow water to collect. I fill the basin with peat moss or some other good mulching material to keep the soil cool in the summer and to protect the roots from alternate freezing and thawing in winter. It's also a good idea to prune back the top branches by about a third to compensate for any damage suffered by the roots during transplanting. Also remove any weak or overlapping branches. Pruning at planting time is especially important with a balled-and-burlapped tree since its roots were no doubt severely pruned at the nursery.

"Help! Help! I'm a $10 tree trapped in a $5 hole!"

A Fair-Skinned Beauty

Now that you've moved your tree into its new home, you must provide it with protection from the elements until it becomes a firmly established member of your family. A young tree, especially a dogwood, beech or maple, has a very delicate complexion—or bark. And it's up to you to keep the tree from getting sunburned. This doesn't mean you have to go out and massage the bark with suntan lotion every day. Just give your tree a "jacket" to protect it from the sun. In other words, wrap the trunk from the base to the lowest branches with burlap, foil, cheesecloth or tree wrap, which is made of waterproof, corrugated paper. Take two firm turns around the base of the tree, then spiral the tape up the trunk, overlapping the layers by about an inch to keep water out. Tie the top and bottom ends of the tape with cotton cord. The wrap should stay on the tree for about 2 years to give the bark time to toughen up.

If you live in a windy section of the country, you may need to stake your tree to keep it standing straight and tall. On opposite sides of the rootball, drive two 6-feet-long stakes about 2 feet into the ground. Make sure the stakes do not pierce the rootball. Take a length of heavy-gauge wire and thread it through a short piece of old garden hose. Loop the wire around the tree, placing the garden hose around the trunk to keep the bark from being cut or bruised by the wire. Attach the ends of the wire to the stakes. Repeat this process on the opposite stake. I usually remove the stakes in about two years—at the same time I remove the tree wrap. By this time, the tree will have planted its feet firmly and will be able to withstand the wind on its own.

However, two stakes may not provide enough support for trees larger than 3 inches in diameter. Instead, drive 3 short stakes into the ground at equal distances around the tree. Thread 3 sturdy wires through pieces of old garden hose. Loop them around the tree

Newly planted trees have tender bark that should be protected from sunscald with tree wrap or a "guard" like the one below.

trunk just above the lowest branch, using the garden hose to protect the bark as before. Attach the wires to the stakes. For maximum support, the wires should run at 45-degree angles. These wires should stay in place for 2 years, too.

A Suit of Armor

Sun and wind aren't the only problems a young tree faces. Rabbits and mice can seriously damage, or even kill, a young tree by gnawing its tender bark. And then there are young boys with lawn mowers. They may not gnaw the bark off trees, but they can inflict a lot of damage with a lawn mower in high gear. The tree wrap will protect your tree from lawn mowers and rodents during its first 2 years, but what then? I suggest giving your tree a suit of armor. Cut a length of 2-foot-wide hardware cloth. This should be large enough to form a cylinder that will stand about 2 inches away from the trunk on all sides. Wrap the hardware cloth around the tree and wire the ends together. If there is a mulch around the tree, push the mesh down into it. If the tree is not mulched and you plan to hand-clip around it, leave the "armor" loose so you can easily raise it.

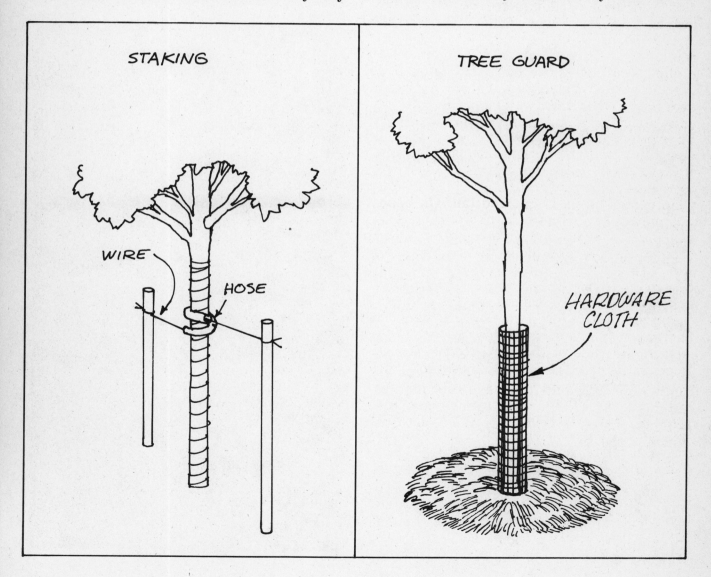

STAKING

WIRE

HOSE

TREE GUARD

HARDWARE CLOTH

Young trees don't need much care to become as vigorous as the ones below. Just give them enough water and use only slow-acting, non-burning fertilizers like the one at left.

I have one more piece of advice on tree planting. Be very careful to use only slow-acting, nonburning fertilizers, such as cottonseed meal, bone meal or slow-release chemical fertilizer, around newly planted trees. My favorite is bone meal. I usually work about ½ cup into the soil I return to the planting hole. From time to time, I also sprinkle a handful of bone meal in the basin around the tree and water it in. Well-rotted manure is also good for working into the planting hole. If you don't mind the looks of it, you can also spread a layer of rotted manure in the basin. Rainwater will leach the nutrients out of the manure and carry them down into the soil.

During your tree's first year, you must make sure it gets enough water. During the growing season, water it once a week unless there's enough rainfall to make this unnecessary. Always take the time to give your tree a long, thirst-quenching drink. Don't just sprinkle the soil surface.

Other than an occasional watering, newly planted trees need no special care. Just talk to them every now and then. Tell them what splendid progress they're making and introduce them to the other trees and plants in your yard. Pretty soon they'll be feeling right at home.

Care

A lot of people forget about a tree once it's planted. I suppose these half-hearted gardeners assume that if trees can survive in a forest with no human help, the trees they've planted in their yards can do the same. And maybe they can. Most trees are tough enough to survive even under adverse growing conditions. But the wise gardener wants much more than survival from his young trees. He wants them to grow into healthy, well-shaped trees and to be beautiful and valuable additions to his landscape.

The wise gardener also knows that trees in the forest are cared for by the world's champion green-thumber, Mother Nature herself. She waters her trees with the purest water available—rainwater. She piles a deep blanket of decomposing leaves, twigs and animal matter around their feet to insulate the soil against extreme heat or cold and to provide them with the nutrients they need. She prunes out dead branches and chops down dead trees with the wind. And she instructs the older trees to protect their younger cousins from the sun and wind.

It's not nice to fool Mother Nature, but it's o.k. to give her a helping hand. And that's exactly what you need to do in your own yard. Since she won't be able to spread a blanket of leaves and other organic matter around the tree, you'll have to help her out by feeding it regularly and perhaps by applying a mulch around it. If Mother Nature's stingy with the rainfall, give that tree a drink yourself. Since your idea of a properly pruned tree is probably different from Mother Nature's, you'll want to take over pruning too. Of course, you can't do anything about sunshine, but don't worry—Mother Nature's been taking care of that department all by herself for a long time.

"Root-feeding trees is too much trouble. I just sprinkle a little fertilizer on the ground and forget about it."

Chow Time

How do you feed a tree? You certainly don't take it a glass of milk and a straw. The milk won't do you any more good than the tree unless you drink it. The milk has to get to your stomach before your body can begin to absorb its nutrients. Obviously, a tree doesn't have a mouth and a stomach, but it does face the same problem that you do. Just as your body can't use the glass of milk while you're holding it in your hand, a tree can't use food unless it's placed within reach of its roots or sprayed directly on its foliage. As you can see, sprinkling fertilizer over the ground beneath a tree is practically useless.

There are two ways to get fertilizer to the roots of a tree—by placing dry fertilizer in holes punched around the tree or by injecting liquid fertilizer into the soil with a special device. You can also spray liquid fertilizer directly onto the foliage.

Fun with Foliar Feeding

Of these three methods, the last, called foliar feeding, is the easiest so I'll explain it first. Foliar feeding also produces the fastest and most dramatic results because the leaves have immediate access to the nutrients. I've seen plain-Jane trees turn into beauty queens radiant with health and pride a week after foliar feeding. They reminded me of the "before" and "after" pictures I've seen in cosmetic advertisements. The ones that

Root feeders are garden hose attachments used to inject a liquid fertilizer solution directly into the soil within a tree's feeding zone. To determine the feeding zone, mark a circle one-third of the way between the trunk and the drip line, then mark another circle an equal distance beyond the drip line. Punch holes evenly over this entire area, spacing them 2 to 3 feet apart.

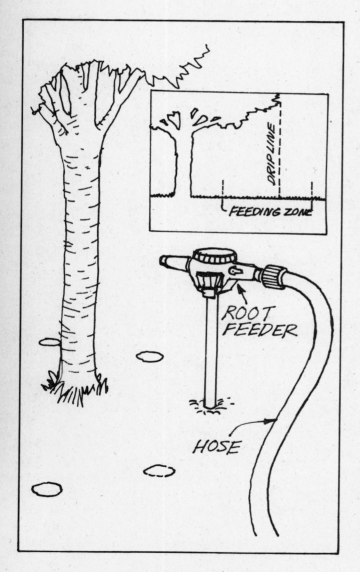

show how Jane Doe, wrinkled, frumpish housewife, turned back the clock with Wanda's Wonder Wrinkle Cream. The "after" picture usually shows an entirely different woman—or maybe Joan Doe, Jane's daughter.

Unlike Wanda's Wonder Wrinkle Cream, foliar feeding does produce truly dramatic effects. Unfortunately, they are not long lasting. Actually, I don't recommend that you use foliar feeding exclusively. If you do, you'll have to feed your trees several times during every growing season. Instead, use foliar feeding to give your trees an occasional beauty treatment—maybe a week before that barbecue you're planning—or to supplement root feeding.

The best tool for foliar feeding is a small, siphon-type sprayer which you attach to your garden hose. Fill the jar (which is about the same size as fruit-canning jars) with concentrated liquid fertilizer. When you turn on the water, the fertilizer will be siphoned up into the hose stream and sprayed out in a diluted form. Because the fertilizer solution will be very diluted, there is no danger of burning the foliage, so you can do your foliar feeding at any time of day. If a tree looks a little gray soon after foliar feeding, don't worry. The leaves are just coated with a film of fertilizer which will wash away in the first rain.

A Shot in the Roots

The easiest way to root feed your trees is to give them an injection. Maybe your doctor has given you vitamin shots. You can do the same thing for your trees. Since no one makes hypodermic needles large enough for trees, you'll have to use a special instrument called an injector, a root feeder, a root-zone applicator or a needle probe. Now don't get me wrong—you're not going to inject fertilizer directly into the tree's trunk. Instead, you're going to squirt liquid nutrients into the soil around the roots.

Root feeders, which can be purchased at most garden centers, are 3 to 4 feet long, hollow, pointed tubes. At the top of the tube is a cylinder into which you place cartridges of concentrated fertilizer and onto which a garden hose is attached.

Before you start root feeding, you must determine the feeding zone of the tree. To do so, mark a circle ⅓ of the way between the trunk of the tree and the drip line. Now mark another circle the same distance beyond the drip line. The area between the circles is the tree's feeding zone and all fertilizer should be placed within it.

If you're using dry fertilizer on a tree, use a crowbar or a soil auger to punch holes one and one-half to two feet apart over the entire feeding zone. Weigh out the proper amount of fertilizer and mix it with an equal quantity of sand, soil or peat moss and funnel about a cup of this mixture into each hole. Cover with soil, sand or peat moss and replace the sod over the hole.

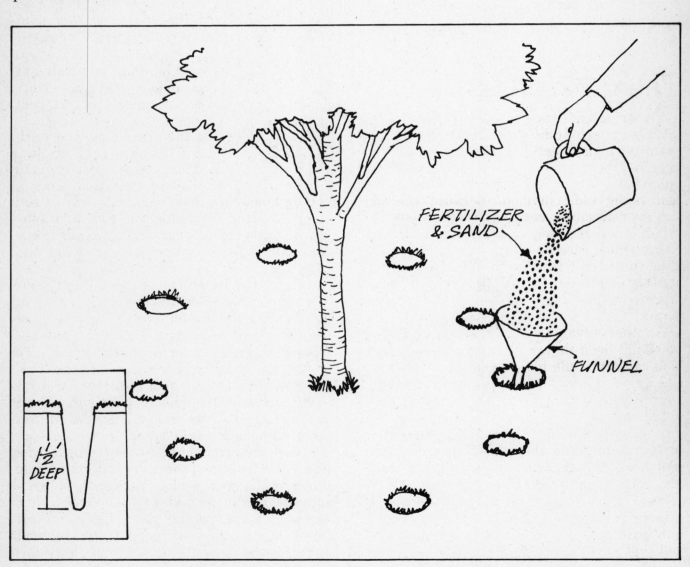

Now turn on the water and insert the pointed end of the root feeder into the soil. Cover the feeding zone evenly, spacing the holes 2 to 3 feet apart. The fertilizer solution will soak into the soil around the tube, thus becoming accessible to many feeder roots. The effects of this type of root feeding are much more long lasting than the effects of foliar feeding. They do not take place as quickly, however.

Because the fertilizer is applied in liquid form, it will drain out of the soil long before the growing season is ended. To keep your trees from getting hungry, you'll have to repeat this sort of root feeding 2 or maybe 3 times during each growing season.

The Hole Story

The tried-and-true method of tree feeding involves punching holes in the soil and filling them with dry fertilizer. This method also involves the most hard work, and it is, in my opinion, still the best method. And I'm not just being old-fashioned. Because the dry fertilizer dissolves very slowly, the results of this method are longer lasting than those of either foliar feeding or injector feeding. Tree roots fed with dry fertilizer won't need another feeding for at least a year. And an afternoon of hard work once a year is not bad at all.

Another advantage of this method is that you don't need to buy any special equipment. You can make the holes with a crowbar or a soil auger if you have one. (A soil auger is simply a giant drill bit with a handle on top.)

I always try to do this type of feeding on a day in early spring. The weather is perfect for gardening and the soil is usually rather moist, which makes punching the holes easier and helps keep the fertilizer from burning the roots. If the soil is dry, I water it thoroughly a few days before I plan to feed my tree. If you wait until the feeding day to water, the soil will be too wet to work in.

Don't just go out and start punching holes in the ground. Get organized first. Start by weighing out your fertilizer. To determine the proper amount, measure the diameter of your tree's trunk. If it is less than 6 inches, weigh out 1 to 2 pounds of dry fertilizer for each inch of diameter. For example, if the diameter of the trunk is 3 inches, you'll need from 3 to 6 pounds of fertilizer. For trees with a diameter greater than 6 inches, use 2 to 4 pounds of fertilizer per inch of diameter. Now mix the fertilizer with an equal amount of sand, soil or peat moss. This, too, helps keep the fertilizer from burning the roots.

Next, mark off the root feeding zone of the tree as described in the previous section on injector feeding. All the feeding holes should be within this area. If you've never root fed a tree, you might want to mark the spots where the holes should be. Plan on making at least 10 holes for every inch of trunk diameter, and space the holes 1½ to 2 feet apart.

If you don't want the grass over the feeding zone to look as if it has caught chicken pox, carefully roll back a small patch of sod with a trowel or shovel before making a feeding hole. Now drive your crowbar or soil auger 1½ to 2 feet into the soil. (To avoid punching a hole in your foot instead of the soil, stand with your feet spread apart and bring the crowbar down between them.) Place a large funnel in the hole and pour about a cup of the fertilizer mixture into it. Try to avoid spilling fertilizer on the lawn or you'll find yourself plagued with tall patches of bright green overfertilized grass. To prevent the grass over the feeding zone from being overfertilized, place a layer of peat moss, soil or sand on top of the fertilizer mixture. Finally, fold down the patch of sod you rolled back earlier and step on it to establish good contact between the roots and soil. Repeat this process until you have covered the entire feeding zone evenly. When you finish, wish your tree "bon appetit," and remind yourself that you won't have to undertake this task again for at least another year.

What's for Lunch?

Now that you know how to feed your trees, you're probably wondering what sort of food they need and like. Take it from me—their favorite dishes are nitrogen, phosphorus and potassium. You can serve these three basic foods a lot of different ways, even organically. You can serve them individually or mixed together in a fertilizer casserole, otherwise known as a complete fertilizer. Before you start planning your menu, though, you'd better learn a little about the food you're going to serve.

Nitrogen promotes rapid growth of the trunk and limbs and the production of lush, dark-green foliage. Phosphorus encourages strong root growth, causes the production of flower buds and increases resistance to cold weather. Potassium is necessary to the production of sugars which increase the tree's resistance to disease and cold. Because it strengthens the tree, potassium also helps to prevent breakage caused by wind, ice and snow. All three of these elements are necessary to a tree's health, but you may from time to time want to emphasize one more than the others. As I said before, I like to use bone meal around newly planted trees because it is nonburning. Because bone meal is high in phosphorus, it also stimulates strong root growth and helps the young tree to become established quickly.

If you want to use an organic fertilizer on larger established trees, I suggest cottonseed meal. It is an excellent nonburning, slow-release fertilizer. Because organic fertilizers are often expensive and hard to find, you may prefer to use one of the many complete chemical fertilizers available at any garden center. These fertilizers are perfectly safe to use on trees if 50 percent or more of the nitrogen content is in slow-release form. If you can't find this information printed on the fertilizer bag, ask the shopkeeper to help you. Is there a bag of leftover lawn fertilizer hidden somewhere under the old newspapers, broken lawn mower blades and miscellaneous junk in your garage? Dig it out and check the label to see if the nitrogen is in

This bag of fertilizer contains 20 percent nitrogen, 4 percent phosphorous, 8 percent potassium and 68 percent inactive carrying agent.

Because organic fertilizers are non-burning, they are excellent to use around trees.

slow-release form, as it is in most good lawn fertilizers. If it is, you can use this fertilizer on your trees and save yourself a trip to the garden center.

Have you ever wondered about those mysterious numbers that appear on every bag of fertilizer? Well, they're not a secret code understood only by an elite circle of fertilizer manufacturers and expert gardeners. They simply indicate the chemical analysis of the fertilizer. A bag of 4-16-4 fertilizer, for example, contains 4 percent nitrogen, 16 percent phosphorus, and 4 percent potassium. (The sum of the numbers is 24; the remaining 76 percent of the fertilizer consists of an inactive carrying agent.) A bag of 8-32-8 formula contains twice the percentage of active elements as the 4-16-4, so you would only have to use half as much.

What's the best formula for trees? There's a lot of controversy on this subject, but I prefer 10-8-6. Some professional gardening writers recommend 7-7-7, and I suppose it's satisfactory, but I like to give my trees a hefty dose of slow-release nitrogen to keep the foliage dense, dark-green and healthy.

So you see, planning a menu for your trees is not difficult. As a matter of fact, my wife says it's a lot easier than planning the week's menu for our family.

When Do We Eat?

There's also a lot of controversy over the proper time to feed a tree. Some people feed their trees in either early spring or late fall—or sometimes both. I strongly disagree with this. In my opinion, early spring is the only time to feed a tree! In the first place, trees wake up ravenously hungry after their long winter naps. Second, if you fertilize a tree in early spring, the nutrients will be available to it throughout most of the growing season. By early fall, the tree will have used up most of the nutrients from its spring meal. But this does not mean you should fer-

CHANGING THE GRADE
AROUND A TREE

If your house sits on a sloping or hilly site, you may at some time decide to level out all or part of your yard. Since levelling involves either digging out or filling in soil, the grade around your trees will be changed.

Should you be raising the soil level, the shallow feeder roots of the tree will be deprived of oxygen by the extra layer of soil, and the tree may die. To prevent this, build a brick or stone well around the tree to maintain the original soil level. The walls of the well should be 4 to 6 feet away from the tree's trunk to give the tree adequate access to oxygen. Piling stones and rubble behind the wall will let still more oxygen into the root area.

If the grade around the tree is being lowered, you'll have to make a raised bed to maintain the original soil level. If you don't, shallow feeder roots will be broken and exposed to the open air during the excavation. The edge of the bed should be halfway between the trunk and the drip line (a line around the perimeter of the foliage.) Some of the surface feeder roots will be damaged when you make the bed, so you should feed and water the tree regularly for a season or two to encourage the formation of new roots.

tilize again! At this point, another dose of nitrogen would encourage the tree to keep on growing vigorously, regardless of the season. The new growth wouldn't have a chance to fully mature before winter set in. Consequently, it would be very susceptible to damage caused by wind, cold and ice.

If you are foliar feeding your trees or root feeding them with an injector, you will have to make several applications of fertilizer during the growing season. Start your fertilization program early in the spring so you will have time to feed the trees several times before midsummer. Then, about the middle of July, stop feeding altogether. I know this sounds cruel but I have your trees' best interests at heart.

Trees Like an Occasional Drink

Unless you live in a very dry section of the country, frequent watering of established trees will probably be unnecessary. The feeder roots of a tree extend deep into the ground and range over a wide area, so the tree has access to underground soil moisture even when the soil surface looks quite dry. During prolonged periods of drought, however, the amount of underground soil moisture is greatly reduced. It is during such

times that you should water the tree. The tree could probably survive the drought without your help, but its growth would slow down and its foliage might become wilted and dull.

As Grandma Putt used to say, "If a job's worth doing, it's worth doing well." This bit of advice is especially applicable to watering trees. Whenever you water a tree, do a thorough job or don't do it at all. The water must be allowed to soak deep into the ground so it will be accessible to the feeder roots. If you haphazardly sprinkle the soil beneath the tree for a few minutes, the water will only soak down a few inches. Repeated shallow watering will cause the tree to develop a shallow root system which will do a poor job of anchoring the tree and of supplying it with moisture and nutrients.

On the other hand, overwatering can eventually cause tree roots to drown and rot. Unfortunately, gardeners with the best of intentions often accidentally overwater their trees regularly and thoroughly, perhaps with an automatic sprinkler system. While their lawns are a lovely, velvety green, their trees are slowly drowning. If you water your lawn regularly, it would be a good idea to check the drainage around your trees. If they're standing with their feet in puddles, you'd better cut back on your lawn-watering program.

Several different types of hoses are suitable for watering trees. You can even use an ordinary garden hose, if you keep the water pressure low. Lay the end on a piece of canvas to break the force of the water and to keep it from boring a hole in the soil. Canvas soaker hoses or perforated plastic hoses are the best types for watering trees. Both provide a slow, steady flow of water that will soak deep into the soil without disturbing the surface. The only disadvantage of using a canvas soaker hose is that it will rot and have to be replaced much sooner than a perforated plastic hose. (Canvas hoses are also more expensive than plastic ones.)

If possible, encircle the tree with a canvas or plastic soaker hose, placing it within the

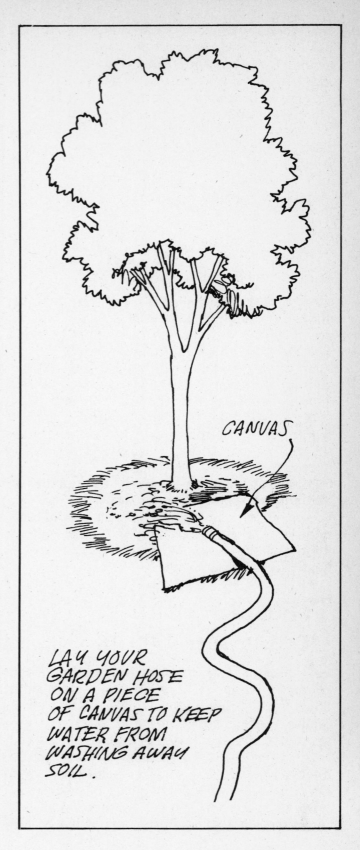

CANVAS

LAY YOUR GARDEN HOSE ON A PIECE OF CANVAS TO KEEP WATER FROM WASHING AWAY SOIL.

root feeding zone. If you're using a plastic hose with holes on only one side, place that side next to the ground so that the water can soak directly into the soil. Turn the water on slowly; at first all you want is a slow trickle. Don't increase the flow of water until the soil is thoroughly soaked to a depth of about 2 feet. Be patient—this may take several hours.

If you don't mind the looks of straw, it makes a fine mulch.

Don't Let Your Trees Get Cold Feet

As you remember, in the chapter on planting, I suggested filling the basin around a newly planted tree with a good organic mulch. Well, newly planted trees aren't the only ones who like a blanket of mulch around their feet. Their older, more established brothers find mulching very beneficial, too.

A mulch is simply a layer of straw or other material, usually organic, which is placed around the base of a tree or other plant. And mulching helps solve a lot of tree raising problems. First, a good, thick mulch kills all the grass and weeds beneath it, which means you can stop hand-clipping around the base of every tree. Second, a mulch holds moisture in the soil and keeps the soil temperature more nearly constant. Third, a mulch insulates the roots against alternate freezing and thawing in winter. Fourth, organic mulches improve the fertility and tilth of the soil as they decompose. Fifth and finally, some mulches are very ornamental in addition to all their other functions.

Many materials, both organic and inorganic, can be used as mulches, but some are too unattractive for use in a home landscape. Straw, chopped corn cobs and black plastic, for example, are all excellent materials for mulching a vegetable garden or an out-of-the-way flower or shrub bed. But I wouldn't suggest using any of these materials to mulch a tree in the middle of your front yard. The mulch would stand out like a sore thumb and detract from the beauty of the tree and of the landscape as a whole.

Instead, use one of the many ornamental mulches. Wood chips, buckwheat hulls, chopped bark, peat moss and stones are among the best. All make neat, clean mulches that will blend into any landscape. If you like, you can use fallen leaves for a natural-looking mulch. (If possible, chop them up.)

It's difficult to say how deep a mulch should be. Some materials, such as sawdust and peat moss, become almost solid as they settle, so you will need less of them than of a coarse, bulky material, such as straw or wood

Chopped bark is one of the best ornamental organic mulches.

"With a blanket of mulch around my feet, I can smile through all life's little ups and downs."

chips. I suggest that you start with 3 to 4 inches of mulch. If grass or weeds poke their naughty heads through the mulch, pull them out and add another layer of mulching material. You will also have to add more mulching material from time to time to replace that which has decomposed.

If you live in an area subject to freezing temperatures during part or all of the winter, you should pile on an extra layer of mulch before the first fall frost. Straw, spoiled hay, manure and salt hay make excellent winter mulches. You can remove these mulches in the spring if they're too unattractive. Or you could camouflage them with a layer of ornamental mulch.

Pruning

From time to time you may have to perform surgery on your trees. If a tree becomes injured or diseased, you will have to do some corrective surgery to save the tree's health—and perhaps its life. At other times you may have to perform purely cosmetic surgery to improve the appearance of the tree or to keep it from intruding in areas where it does not belong. It's a good idea, for example, to remove any branches that are too low to comfortably walk under. Maybe there's a low-branched tree standing between your living room window and a spectacular view; a little judicious pruning might allow you to enjoy the view without sacrificing the tree.

Performing surgery is a serious business. No reputable surgeon would perform an operation unless it was absolutely necessary.

Likewise, you should not do any unnecessary pruning. Once you cut off a limb, there's nothing you can do to make it grow back. Of course, all injured or diseased branches should be removed immediately to prevent decay or disease from spreading throughout the tree. If you're pruning to improve the beauty of the tree, make sure the alterations you're planning will be improvements. Don't randomly hack out branches and then stand back to survey the overall effect. Instead, study the tree before you prune it. Try to visualize the way the tree will look after the pruning is done. Look at the structure of the tree and try to pick out its best features. Could its profile be improved by pruning? Or does it have an interesting branch pattern that could be made more dramatic by pruning out some of the smaller branches?

Scheduling the Operation

Trees can be pruned at any time during the year. I always schedule pruning for early spring so my trees will have an entire growing season to heal their wounds. However, some trees should not be pruned in early spring. Flowering trees which formed their flower buds during the previous growing season should not be pruned in early spring because this would greatly reduce the number of blossoms produced that year. Instead, postpone pruning until after the tree has flowered. Before pruning any flowering tree, find out when it sets its blossoms. If you time your pruning properly, you won't miss a single season of bloom.

Beeches, birches, maples, walnuts and yellowwoods should not be pruned in spring. If you do, they'll bleed all over your pruning tools and your lawn. This bleeding, or exuding sap, is not really dangerous to the tree, but it is messy and unattractive. It's best to prune these trees in late summer or early fall when the sap isn't flowing so freely.

"I told you I'd belt you if you cut off one more limb."

The Tools of the Trade

Amateur tree surgeons often make the mistake of trying to make do with the tools they already have instead of purchasing tools made especially for pruning. Do not try to prune trees with your hedge clippers. And don't use an ordinary carpenter's saw to cut off large branches. Its fine teeth will stick in live wood. The coarser teeth of a pruning saw are designed to cut cleanly through live wood.

In addition to a pruning saw, which you'll use to remove large limbs, you'll need a pair of long-handled lopping shears for smaller branches. A pruning knife is ideal for cleaning up the rough edges of pruning cuts, but any sharp knife will do. Buy a can of tree paint for treating all wounds larger than an inch in diameter. Do not under any circumstances use ordinary house paint; it may kill your tree.

How do you prune those limbs high above your head? You could climb the tree, but there's an easier and safer way. You can lop off small branches, less than one inch in diameter, with a handy tool called a pole pruner. The pole pruner is, obviously, mounted on top of a long pole, and its blades

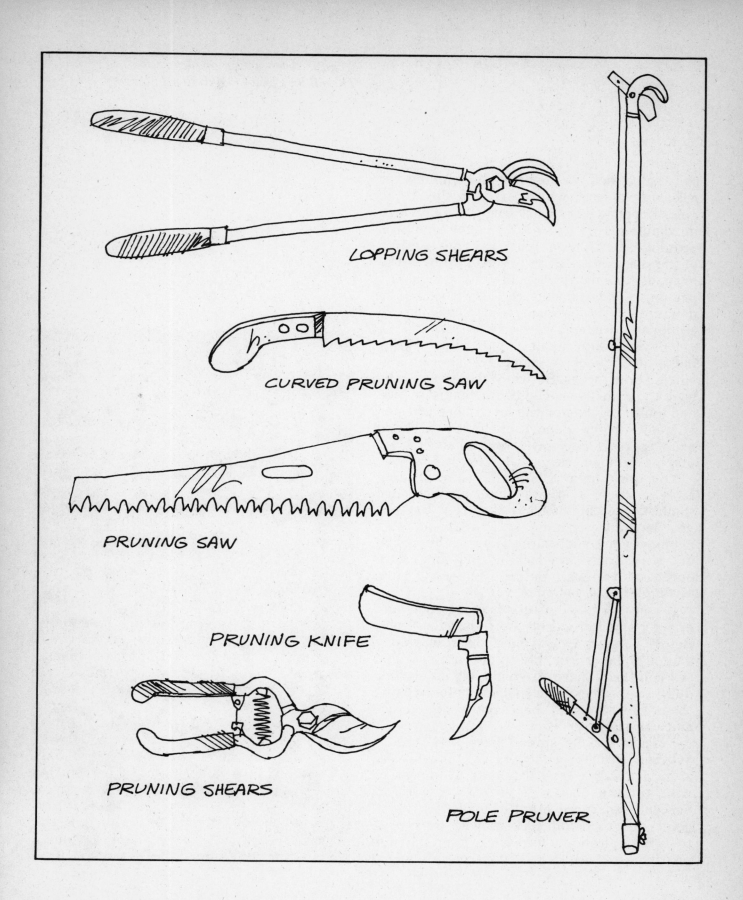

LOPPING SHEARS

CURVED PRUNING SAW

PRUNING SAW

PRUNING KNIFE

PRUNING SHEARS

POLE PRUNER

*Always buy quality pruning tools.
They'll last longer and do a better
job.*

can be closed or opened by pulling or releasing a cord which extends down the pole. To remove branches larger than an inch in diameter, you'll need a pole-mounted pruning saw. These tools can be used to prune branches 12 to 18 feet above the ground. An amateur should not try to do any pruning above this height, as it could be dangerous. Professional tree surgeons are equipped to handle this sort of task.

I have nothing against chainsaws. They make quick work of chopping firewood and cutting down trees. But they should never be used to prune trees. Holding a chainsaw high enough to reach even the lowest branches on a tree is very dangerous. Stick to hand pruning tools and save your chainsaw for playing lumberjack.

You don't have to buy all your pruning tools at once. Just buy them as you need them. Or you might borrow or rent tools. If you have a neighbor who does his own pruning, you could share tools with him. Find out what tools he's lacking and limit your purchases to those. Before long, you'll have a complete set between you.

If you buy good-quality pruning tools and care for them properly, they'll last for years. Before you put away your tools, always dry and oil them thoroughly to prevent rust and to keep them sharp. If your tools do become dull, have them sharpened before using them. Dull saws and shears make ragged cuts and can cause bruises.

Disease can be spread from one tree to another by dirty pruning tools. Immediately after pruning a tree that may be diseased, wipe off the blades of your tools with 70 percent denatured ethyl alcohol. It's also a good idea to disinfect borrowed or rented tools with alcohol before using them on your own trees.

At planting time, cut back all the top branches by about a third to compensate for damage to the roots during transplanting. Also remove any weak or overlapping branches.

Surgical Procedures

A young tree should receive its first pruning on the day you plant it in your yard. As I explained earlier, the purpose of this first pruning is to compensate for any damage suffered by the roots during transplanting. The second pruning, which should occur about a year after the first one, will have a lot to do with the appearance of the tree at maturity. The purposes of this pruning are to improve the shape and beauty of the tree and to strengthen it.

Start by cutting out all suckers. These are fast-growing sprouts which may appear at the base of the tree or on some of the branches. Suckers are usually small enough to be removed with a pair of lopping shears. Next, remove any low-hanging branches which will eventually interfere with your activities. None of the branches should be so low that they'll slap you in the face when you walk under the tree. Also check to see if there are any downward-pointing branches which will cause problems as they grow. If there are any, remove them.

A tree with a single trunk is structurally much stronger than one with two or more competing trunks. Because a competing trunk usually grows up at a very sharp angle to the main trunk, the joint between the two is almost always weak. As the trunks grow, a layer of bark will slowly grow down between them, making the problem worse. Eventually

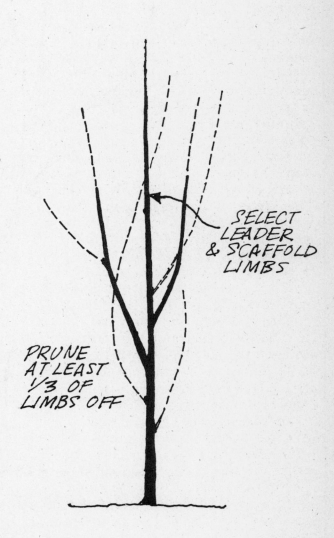

SELECT LEADER & SCAFFOLD LIMBS

PRUNE AT LEAST 1/3 OF LIMBS OFF

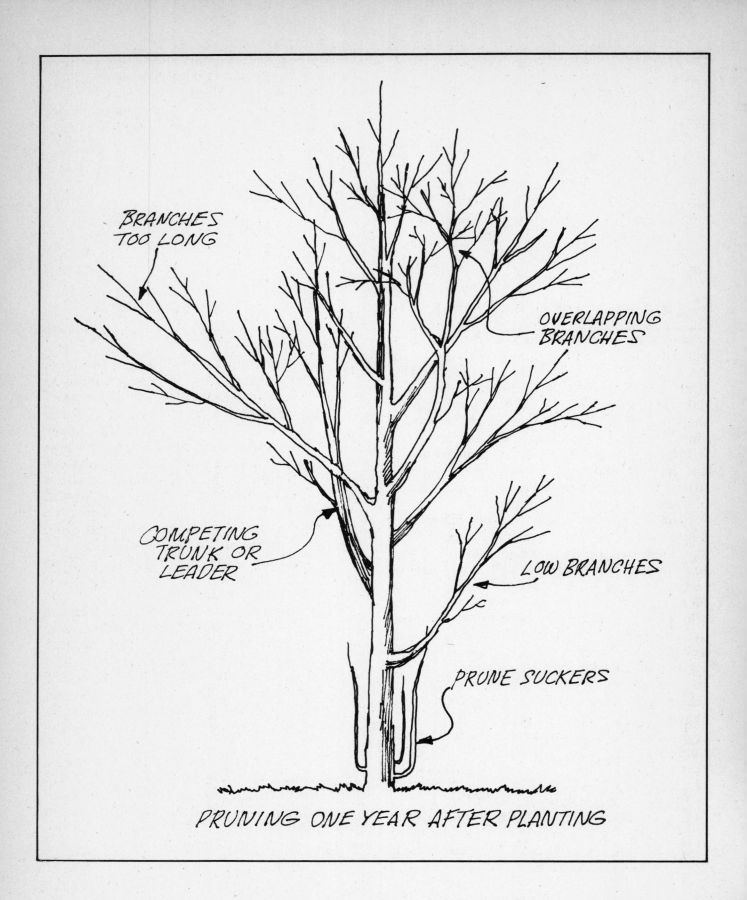

BRANCHES TOO LONG

OVERLAPPING BRANCHES

COMPETING TRUNK OR LEADER

LOW BRANCHES

PRUNE SUCKERS

PRUNING ONE YEAR AFTER PLANTING

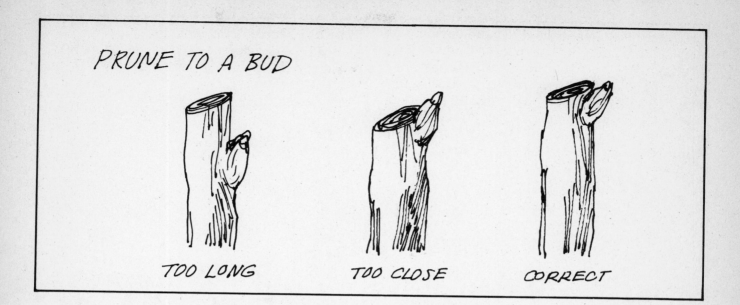

PRUNE TO A BUD

TOO LONG   TOO CLOSE   CORRECT

Your tree certainly won't have as many problems as the one at left, but you may have to do quite a bit of corrective and preventive pruning. If you want to change the shape of a tree, cut back each branch to just beyond a bud pointing in the direction you want new growth to take. Don't leave a stub which might rot, but don't cut too close to the bud either.

the trunks may split apart, ruining the tree. As soon as you notice a branch which looks as if it may become a competing trunk, remove it. If you wait too long, the symmetry of the tree will be affected. Now look at the upper branches and decide which will make the best main limbs. Consider strength as well as beauty. A limb that joins the trunk at a sharp angle is weaker than a more nearly horizontal limb. So if you have a choice between two branches, remove the branch with the narrowest crotch.

Prune back excessively long branches that spoil the symmetry or outline of a tree. The pyramidal hornbeam, for example, is naturally tall and columnar. To emphasize its dramatic beauty, you should shorten any long, irregular branches that spoil its neat outline. Before cutting the branch, look for a bud that points in the direction you want new growth to take. Make a diagonal cut just beyond this bud. Don't leave a stub; it will die and may spread decay through the rest of the branch.

At the top of the tree, you will see one or more leaders, or tall, vertical stems that will form the main trunks. Unless the tree happens to be one of those naturally grown with multiple trunks, such as a birch, shorten all but one of the leaders.

Hopefully, your tree won't have all the

problems I've mentioned. If, however, you decide that you're going to have to do a lot of pruning, it would be a good idea to postpone some of it for a few months. Too much pruning at one time will leave a lot of unsightly wounds and will expose too many areas to fungi and disease. It may also stimulate the production of suckers.

This limb should have been removed long ago before decay and disease could spread to the main trunk as it has now.

Cosmetic Surgery

If you do a good job of pruning a tree while it's young, you probably won't have to do much later on. Of course, you may have some large trees that have never been properly pruned. And these trees may have a lot of serious problems. If so, you have a lot of work ahead of you. Those poor, neglected trees need your help. With proper pruning, you can turn a bedraggled, unkempt tree into a handsome and dignified member of your family. And will he ever thank you! Trees like to look chic and well-groomed just as much as you do.

What do you look for? First, remove any dead, dying or diseased branches. Then look for any wounds in the bark. If your home has just been built, the trees around it may have been seriously damaged by construction equipment. Treating these wounds should be one of the first things you do after moving in. Using a mallet and chisel, cut out the damaged area. Chisel out an elliptical piece of bark. (It should look like an egg standing on end.) Make the ends of the ellipse sharp-pointed and trim off all loose bark. Use your pruning knife to make the edges neat and clean. The shape of this cut prevents water from standing in the wound and promotes faster healing.

I often cover very large wounds with polyethylene to keep out water and to encourage rapid healing. If you don't use polyethylene, paint all exposed wood with a good tree paint. Remember that if water comes in contact with any wood left exposed, rot may eventually develop and spread to the heart of the tree.

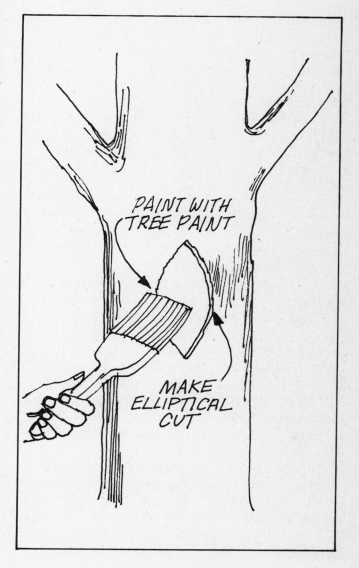

PAINT WITH TREE PAINT

MAKE ELLIPTICAL CUT

Some of your trees may be draped with vines. Maybe even poison ivy. Even if the vines are still small, it's best to remove them. If you don't, they'll eventually grow so large that they choke your tree to death. To get rid of poison ivy, first put on a pair of old, heavy gloves, then use a saw to cut off each vine at ground level. Throw out the gloves or wash them thoroughly and clean the saw so you won't catch poison ivy the next time you use it. A year later, remove the dead brittle vines.

You may notice slimy, stagnant water oozing from the bark or from a crotch of the tree. This is usually a sign that excess water has built up in the center, or heartwood of the tree and is causing pressure. To relieve this pressure, drill 2 or 3 holes at upward angles in the vicinity of the oozing. Insert a pipe in each hole to insure good drainage and to prevent discoloration of the bark.

If a tree has exposed roots, you can easily detect "girdling roots," or roots that cross over others. Another sign of girdling roots is a trunk with no natural flare at the base (or on one side of the base). If girdling roots are not removed, they may eventually strangle the tree. Saw through the root as close to the trunk as possible, being careful not to damage other roots or the trunk. If there are several girdling roots, remove only one or two. The rest can be removed in about two years.

Now look at the branches. Some may hang too low. Others may have narrow, weak crotches. Before you remove a branch, try to visualize how the tree will look without it. If removal will spoil the tree's appearance, try to think of less drastic solutions. You can sometimes give a low-hanging limb a lift by pruning out some of the smaller branches to lighten its burden.

If one branch constantly rubs against another, a wound will eventually develop in the bark of one or both branches. And it will be an open invitation to insects and diseases. Decide which branch contributes least to the good looks of the tree and remove it.

"My 24-hour living girdle is killing me!"

60

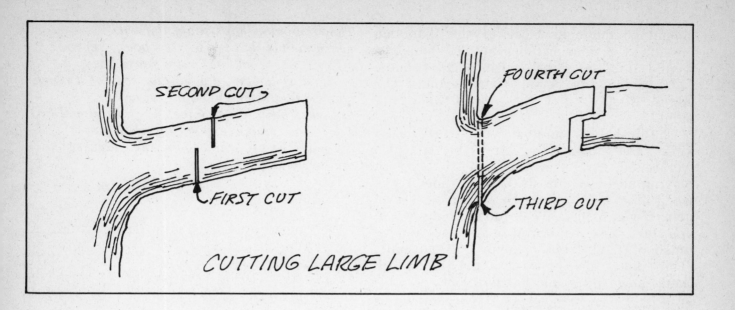

SECOND CUT

FIRST CUT

CUTTING LARGE LIMB

FOURTH CUT

THIRD CUT

Amputating a Large Limb

I'm sure everybody's seen enough Saturday-morning cartoons to know that you shouldn't sit on the end of a limb you're sawing off. But you may not know the correct way to remove large limbs. If you just make one cut from the top of the branch to the bottom, before you finish cutting, the branch may fall of its own weight and rip off a long strip of bark and wood from the trunk.

To avoid such a catastrophe, first make a short upward cut about 2 feet away from the trunk. A few inches nearer the end of the branch, make a downward cut. Keep sawing until the branch breaks off.

But you're not finished yet. If you leave a stub, the wound will never heal properly. In order for healing to take place, the cambium, a cell-producing layer beneath the bark, must grow over the exposed area. The cambium cannot grow up and over the edge of a stub, so the end of the stub will decay, and this decay can spread to the very heart of the tree.

To remove the stub, make a shallow cut up from the underside. Then finish cutting through the stub from the top. Both cuts

To remove a large limb, first make a short, upward cut about 2 feet away from the trunk. A few inches farther out on the branch, cut downward until the limb breaks off. Remove the stub by making a short upward cut, then a long downward cut, both flush with the trunk.

should be made as close to the trunk as possible. Use your pruning knife to shape the wound into an ellipse with pointed ends. Clean away any ragged bark around the edges. Finally paint the wound with tree paint.

The first time you go at your trees with a knife and saw, they may be a little frightened. But after they see that you're playing surgeon, not Jack the Ripper, they won't mind nearly so much. Of course, it also helps if you explain what you're doing before you start. Most important of all, when you've finished, thank them for being good patients. (They didn't kick or scream, did they?) Tell them how much nicer they look.

The tree below has been pollarded, which means that the top has been sheared off so the tree will put out a dense head of slender shoots. To pollard a tree, let it reach about 8 feet in height, then cut all the branches back to 2 to 5 feet long. They will callus over, and every spring when you cut back the branches again, the calluses will become larger.

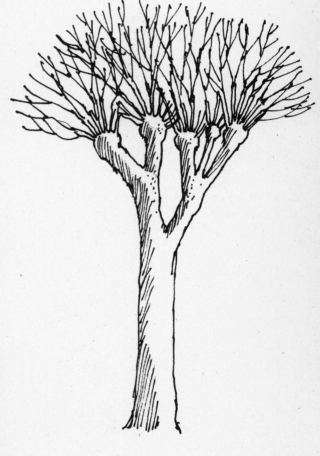

*Removing the small, twiggy branches from the
lower limbs of a tree often reveals the
strength and beauty of its branching pattern.
This high pruning also allows more
light to fall on the lawn.*

This tree is a perfect example of poorly planned, excessive pruning. Structural faults, such as multiple trunks and weak crotches, were left uncorrected.

PALMS

If you live in Florida, California or one of the warmer southern states, you can add the exotic tropical beauty of palms to your landscape. Basically there are 2 types of palms — those with fan-shaped leaves 3 feet or more wide and those with leaves shaped like giant feathers. Most palms are tropical trees or shrubs, but some can stand temperatures as low as 20° F. Among the hardier fan palms are the Mediterranean fan palm, the Mexican blue palm, the palmettos and the needle palm. Hardy feather palms include the queen palm, the slate palm and the Chilean wine palm.

However, no palm can survive winter outdoors in the North. If you do live in a cold climate, don't despair. You can still grow palms indoors or in a greenhouse. Most make excellent tub plants. All they require is good, rich soil and plenty of fertilizer and moisture. When the weather warms up, you can move your palms onto the patio or porch for the summer. They will look nice alone or as a background for tropical-looking flowering plants, such as a bougainvillea vine or a potted citrus tree.

Pests

The best way to keep from getting sick is to stay healthy. That may sound like a useless piece of advice, but think about it for a minute. If you eat the right foods, get enough rest and generally take care of yourself, you'll feel good and you probably won't be spending a lot of time in a doctor's office. Of course, if you do occasionally get sick, you should do something about it as soon as possible.

The best way to keep your trees free of insects and diseases is to keep them healthy too. If a problem does arise, do something about it before it becomes serious. Proper pruning and adequate feeding and watering all contribute to a tree's resistance to disease. So does keeping the area around it clean and free of rubble that may harbor insects and diseases.

"You won't like me. I have a very sour disposition."

BOX ELDER BUGS

These narrow, ½-inch-long insects are brownish black with 3 lengthwise red stripes on the thorax. Their wings are red-veined. They feed on the flowers, foliage, fruits and twigs of box elders, ashes and other trees. These obnoxious, ugly bugs will also move right into your home.

To control box elder bugs, spray with chlordane, diazinon or malathion.

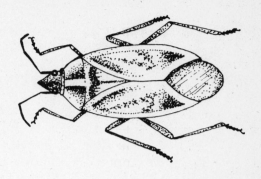

ELM LEAF BEETLES

Elm leaf beetles are about ¼ inch long and light yellow or brownish green in color. They have black spots on the head and thorax and a black or slate-colored stripe along the outer margins of the wing covers. As their name suggests, these insects feed on the foliage of elm trees. Their presence is signified by skeletonized leaves or leaves riddled with large holes.

To control these pests, spray immediately with Sevin or chlordane. Treating the trunk is also helpful.

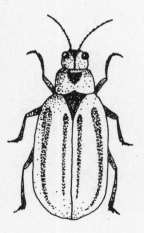

BORERS

Borers are difficult to detect because they feed inside the twigs, branches, trunks and roots of many trees. If you look closely at a borer-infested tree, you will probably notice small holes with sawdust around them. Newly planted trees and sickly trees are particularly vulnerable to borers, and a tree riddled with borers' holes has little chance of surviving. The dogwood and pecan are both particularly subject to attack from borers.

Wrapping the trunks of newly planted trees with tree wrap will keep borers from laying eggs on the bark. In midspring, spray established trees 4 times with methoxychlor at weekly intervals. If a tree is already badly infested with borers, insert wires into their holes to kill them or inject a pest killer containing lindane.

Change the Oil Once a Year

The best way to keep insects from damaging your trees is to stop them before they get a foot in the door. And dormant oil sprays will do just this. These sprays are available at most garden centers, and, because they consist mainly of mineral oil, they will not harm birds or animals. Dormant oil sprays work by coating and smothering insect eggs, so they must be applied before the eggs have a chance to hatch. The proper time for dormant spraying is in early spring

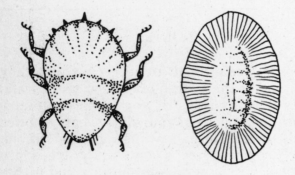

SCALE INSECTS

Male scales are harmless to trees, but females can kill a whole tree by sucking its sap with their long, needlelike feeding tubes. These insects vary in size from one-eighth to one-half inch. The females are wingless and, after crawling around for a time, they insert their beaks into a twig or branch and stay where they are for life. Some scales have soft bodies, others have a waxy shell, and still others have hard, armored bodies. Some scales also secrete honeydew which attracts sooty-mold fungus.

Spray trees infested with scale with dormant oil in early spring. This smothers both the female scales and their eggs. Trees to which oil is harmful (such as Japanese and sugar maples) should be sprayed with malathion when the newly hatched scales are in the crawling stage in early summer. Spray 2 more times at intervals of about 2 weeks.

APHIDS

Aphids, or plant lice, are seldom larger than one-eighth of an inch. They suck the juices out of leaves, stems and buds, and are particularly fond of succulent new growth. They often crowd onto new, growing twigs and cause a malformation of the foliage. Aphids themselves don't really harm trees, but they do spread disease and secrete honeydew which attracts sooty-mold fungus.

Unless the infestation is severe, just blast the aphids off the trees with a hard jet of water from a garden hose or release a handful of ladybugs at the base of the tree. If more severe measures are necessary, spray with pyrethrum or malathion. Before the trees leaf out the following spring, spray with dormant oil to prevent the aphids' returning.

before the buds start to open. If for some reason you can't spray in early spring, you can still use a delayed dormant oil spray, which should be applied immediately after the tree is fully leafed out.

Do not use oil sprays on or near evergreens. Some oil sprays should not be used on maples; ask your nurseryman to recommend one that won't harm your maples. Also avoid using oils sprays when the temperature is below 50 degrees or above 80 degrees. They won't work in cold weather and they may burn leaves in very hot weather.

You can apply dormant or other sprays

LEAF MINERS

There are many types of leaf miners; all feed between the two leaf surfaces. All the different leaf miners seem to have a favorite host. Birch trees are plagued by the birch leaf miner, the larva of a black sawfly. The miners make large brown blisters and blotches on the leaves, giving the whole tree a blighted appearance. The birch is most vulnerable to miners, but other susceptible trees are black locusts, elms, hawthorns, lindens, oaks and poplars.

As soon as the leaves begin to unfold in spring, spray with diazinon, dimethoate, carbaryl or malathion. Spray twice again at 10-day intervals. About 5 weeks after the last spraying, repeat the whole treatment, again spraying 3 times at 10-day intervals.

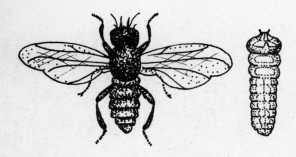

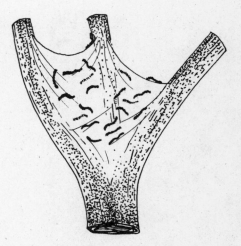

CATERPILLARS

Caterpillars are the worm-like larvae of moths and butterflies. They may be smooth or fuzzy and come in many different sizes and colors. All caterpillars love to dine on foliage, flowers and sometimes fruit. Cankerworms, also known as inchworms, hatch in spring and can deface or defoliate a tree very rapidly. Leaf rollers and tent caterpillars are even more destructive.

Except on Japanese maples, sugar maples and similar trees, a dormant oil spray is the best remedy for a caterpillar invasion. Where dormant oil can't be used, spray in spring and midsummer with carbaryl, methoxychlor, Sevin or Bacillus thuringiensis, which is a bacterial insecticide.

Dutch elm disease is gradually killing off some of our most beautiful shade trees, as you can see below.

with the same garden-hose attachment used for foliar feeding. With average water pressure, these sprayers can reach a height of 25 to 30 feet. You'll need help from a professional tree man if you want to spray taller trees.

Dormant oil sprays aren't the only ecologically sound insect control measures available to you. Mother Nature has come up with a few good ones herself, and she'll be happy to share them with you. Ladybugs are lovely little creatures and they have a huge appetite for aphids. Aphid lions ferociously gobble up aphids, scale and lots of other tree-damaging insects. Praying mantises, those strange-looking green insects, make

This wound should have been cleaned up before tree paint was applied. As you can see, very little healing has taken place.

Professional tree men should be called in to spray trees taller than 20 to 25 feet.

quick work of aphids, flies and various kinds of beetles. All these industrious insects can be purchased from insect breeders catering to organic gardeners.

Weapons for the War on Pests

Even if you follow all the rules of good tree care, you may occasionally be faced with a full-scale insect invasion. Then it is time to turn to some of the more potent chemical weapons in your anti-insect arsenal. I've listed some of your main insect enemies and the weapons you should use against them. Whenever you use chemical sprays, follow the manufacturer's instructions exactly. Try not to spray at a time when birds are nesting. When you finish spraying, clean your equipment thoroughly and store all sprayers and leftover chemicals out of the reach of pets, children and careless adults.

Guide to Shade Trees

ALDER (Alnus)

The largest and most important tree of this family is the black alder of Europe. It was introduced successfully in America during colonial times and grows well in our northeastern states. From here it has spread and become naturalized in many sections.

The black alder sometimes reaches 70 feet in height and has a trunk 3 feet in diameter. The handsome foliage is a deep, dark green and somewhat sticky as the leaves unfold in the spring. The flowers are greenish or yellowish catkins and the fruits are small, woody cones.

One of the best uses for alders is in hedges along the borders of streams where their interlacing roots keep the banks from crumbling and keep the current clear in midstream.

The seaside alder also occurs on stream banks and is a small tree or a large shrub with a trunk up to 5 inches in diameter. The narrow head is round-topped and made up of small zig-zag branchlets.

It is an attractive little tree with oblong, finely-toothed, shiny leaves.

The male flowers are slender catkins 2 to 3 inches long and the female flowers are tiny, cone-like flowers. The fruit is cone-like with many scales, and dark brown or nearly black in color. They mature in late summer or early fall.

The Oregon or red alder reaches a height of 80 feet, even exceeding the black alder in size. It has smooth, pale-gray bark reminiscent of the beech. The flowers and cone fruits are very large.

AMUR CORK TREE
(Phellodendron amurense)

The amur cork tree is so named because it has corky bark. It may grow 30 to 40 feet tall but in cultivation it is usually somewhat smaller. The leaves are often 10 to 15 inches long and are composed of 5 to 11 leaflets.

The amur cork tree thrives in loamy soil and is a good specimen tree when planted where it will have ample room and need not compete with larger and more vigorous trees. It is an excellent lawn tree and complements a low modern style home where a taller tree would seem out of place.

The only difficulty in pruning this tree is experienced when it is quite young. There is a tendency for it to form dual leaders. One trunk must be chosen and trained to form a definite trunk, even though this trunk may be quite short. The pruning should be done in summer.

Young plants may be easily raised from

seeds that have been washed free of the fleshy material surrounding them. Seeds should be sown in a cold frame in a sheltered place outdoors. Pot them up singly when they are large enough to handle. When they are large enough, plant them in a nursery border.

ASH (Fraxinus)

Ash trees when fully grown are large and stately with smooth trunks. The bark is often checked into small, diamond-shaped plates, giving the tree a handsome appearance even during the winter months. As shade trees, ashes are highly desirable; as timber trees they are very valuable.

The white ash is possibly the most noble tree in the American forest, taller even than an oak or a walnut. Graceful and slim as a young tree, it strengthens as it approaches maturity. In the forest it usually forms a narrow head, but as a specimen planted on the home grounds, the dome of the white ash is broad and symmetrical. The bark varies in color from a light gray to a dark brown. The leaves are from 8 to 12 inches long and have from 5 to 9 sharp-pointed leaflets, dark green and smooth above, pale green beneath.

The flowers are of two kinds on different trees, the male in dense reddish-purple clusters and the female in more open bunches. The fruit of the ash is winged, 1 to 1 ½-inches long, resembling the blade of a canoe paddle in outline, with the seed at the handle end. The fruits, which mature in late summer, are widely distributed by the wind.

ASH, BLACK

If given a choice, the black ash prefers to grow on marshy land but will obligingly accommodate itself to other types of soil. It is a somberly handsome tree. In winter its buds are blue-black, in summer its foliage is a deep green, and its bark and wood are both dark-colored.

The leaves are long and pointed and at maturity are a foot or more in length.

The seedpods of the black ash are borne in open panicles 8 to 10 inches long and each

WHITE ASH

one contains a single short, flat seed.

Black ash wood is tough, heavy and coarse-grained. The Indians used black ash splints to weave baskets.

As a lawn tree, the black ash often dies of thirst, but it will do very well if you have a low, marshy area on your land where other trees will not grow.

ASH, BLUE

This is a handsome member of the family often cultivated in the parks and gardens of the Eastern states. Quick-growing and hardy, it is nearly impervious to many of the ills that beset other trees. It will, in a favorable environment, reach a height of 120 feet, holding its head above a slender trunk and small, spreading branches. The bark is light gray tinged with red, irregularly divided into large, plate-like scales.

ASH, RED

The red ash is found along valleys and stream banks where it often attains a height of 30 to 60 feet. It is highly valued in eastern sections both as a shade tree and for ornament.

The head is compact with twiggy, slender branches. The twigs are pale and hairy at first, but with age the hairs, which often stay on 2 or 3 years, turn a rusty brown. Eventually the twig becomes smooth.

The leaves are 4 to 6 inches long, lustrous, light yellow green above and pale and silky beneath. The small flowers appear late in the spring, as the leaves begin to unfold. Male and female flowers appear on separate trees. Red ash seeds are extremely long and slender and have very graceful outlines.

BEECH (Fagus)

This tree, widely distributed, is one of the most beautiful and useful in America. It grows from the Great Lakes to the Gulf of Mexico, from Florida to Texas and from New England to Wisconsin. And wherever the beech trees grow, they are likely to form great forests.

Beeches like the slopes of mountains and rich river bottoms. Some of the largest specimens grow in the basin of the lower Ohio River and on the sunny slopes of the Alleghany Mountains.

A beech is beautiful and interesting enough to stand alone and, with room for full development, will make a fine-shaped symmetrical tree. The branches are horizontal or slightly drooping and thickly set with slender, flexible twigs. The tree has many limbs, and the trunk is stout, supporting a conical or round head with exceedingly dense foliage. It is a marvelous tree for shade and may grow as tall as 120 feet with a diameter of 3 to 4 feet—a truly impressive sight when fully mature.

The bark of the beech is smooth, unfurrowed, and pale gray. The blotches that mark it are of even a paler hue.

In summer, the leaves of the beech are its greatest attraction. In spring these leaves are closely plaited and covered with a silvery down. Then, seemingly in a day, the fuzz disappears completely and the full-grown leaves become apparent. And they are beautiful—thin, feather-veined, uniformly green and saw-toothed. The leaves hang on the trees well and keep their good green color all through the summer, turning in autumn to pale gold. This gold does not tarnish and the leaves cling to the tree for a very long time, often until the end of winter.

The beech tree does bloom, but the delicate flowers fade very quickly. The tassels drop rapidly and are followed by the prickly burrs of the forming nuts. The burrs open with the first frosts, their 4 sides falling apart. The beechnuts are sweet and nutritious and much liked by many dwellers of the forest. Man himself used them for food long ago when he lived in caves. Beechnuts are small in size, but the rich, delicate flavor more than makes up for this. In pioneer America, hogs were turned loose at times to eat the beechnuts in the forest, and the flesh from such animals was said to be of superior flavor.

Beechnuts propagate the trees and many young beeches will grow up around a parent tree. Young seedlings do well in the shade of other trees, so each fruiting tree may become the "mother" of many young ones, and thus a beech forest is born.

BIRCH (Betula)

The birches are exceedingly graceful, and if I were asked for a word to sum up the characteristics of these trees, I would say "cheerful."

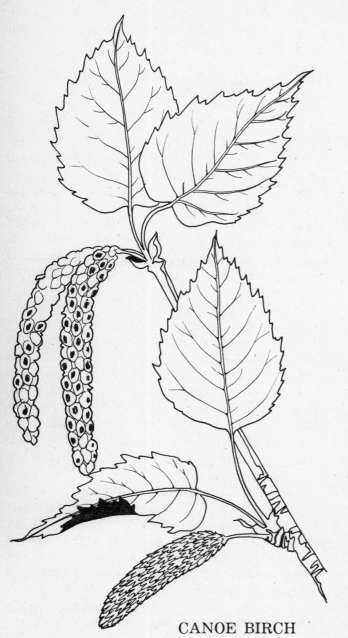

CANOE BIRCH

THE CANOE BIRCH

Probably the most interesting, and certainly the most famous in song and story, is the canoe birch. It has been used as a source of food, drink, transport and lodging by all the forest dwellers. A sweet syrup can be made from its sap and a meal made by drying and grinding the inner bark. The partridges love to feed on the buds and catkins, and the outer bark can be ripped off during warm weather and made into a durable, waterproof covering for canoes. The bark also was used to roof small houses.

THE YELLOW BIRCH

The yellow birch is a timber tree of considerable size and value. It grows from New England to Minnesota and south along the Appalachian range. It may be recognized by the yellow color beneath its shaggy gray bark.

Other interesting members of the birch family are the red birch and the cherry birch. Birches are beautiful but they are not very long-lived. On the home grounds, birches are especially attractive if planted in clumps of 3 to 5.

CATALPA

Catalpas grow well in the United States, but their family hails from the tropics where it includes some 500 trees, shrubs and vines. Catalpas make excellent shade trees and are becoming increasingly popular as they become better known. Handsomely ornamental, they are attractive for either street planting, home grounds or parks.

Catalpas are characterized by large, heart-shaped leaves, spotted white flowers and bean-like seedpods. The bark is scaly and red-brown in color. Catalpas are very fast growing, and for this reason are good to plant where a shade tree is desired in a short time. The wood is coarse but durable, and is used for posts, poles and fences.

Catalpas will grow and do well in ordinary well-drained garden soil, but thrive best in deep, loamy soil where they will grow much larger and more rapidly. Young trees are best

CATALPA

planted in spring or early fall. Select a sunny position if possible.

Catalpas may be propagated by seeds sown in a coldframe, greenhouse or even outdoors. Cuttings made of the ends of half-woody, non-flowering shoots can be easily rooted in summer.

Little pruning is required, but when the trees are young, try to maintain a straight leading shoot by cutting off any side branches which may interfere with such development. Old trees should have any weak, worn-out or dead branches removed. It's best to do this in late summer.

CHESTNUT, CHINESE
(Castanaea mollissima)

Chestnut trees once graced the forests of North America, but then a devastating blight made its appearance, and they have suffered almost complete extinction.

Until its disappearance the American chestnut was one of the most valuable trees in the world, first for the production of its large delicious nuts and second for its very useful and beautiful wood. It was also much planted and admired as a specimen tree for homes and parks.

Because the tree is so valuable, hybridizers have been making crosses between our native American chestnuts and the blight-resistant Chinese and Japanese varieties. Sometimes sucker growths still appear in the wild from the bases of old American chestnuts and occasionally survive the blight long enough to produce nuts. There is hope that the American chestnut will again be a valuable nut-producing tree in the areas where it flourished not so long ago.

Chestnuts are best propagated by seeds (nuts), and the named commercial fruiting varieties are propagated by grafting in the spring on these seedling trees. Sow the seeds as soon as possible after the nuts have ripened, planting them out of doors in drills about an inch deep. If this is not feasible in the autumn, they should be stored in sand and planted the following spring.

BUCKEYE
CHESTNUT

CHESTNUT, HORSE (Aesculus)

Who would not love the shade of a "spreading chestnut tree?" Horse chestnuts, or "buckeyes" as they are often called, are exceedingly attractive trees, useful for planting on large lawns where they may grow to their full potential. The common horse chestnut is most widely used for this purpose. You can recognize it easily by its leaves, which resemble fingers, and its flowers which vary from rosy white through shades of creamy yellow to rosy pink and crimson.

This tree may be planted at any time convenient during fall or spring, but the weather should be mild and the ground not too wet. They like to have their feet in a deep, well-drained loam, cool and moist rather than dry, but will grow in any good garden soil if it is well prepared. Their abundant, fibrous roots make transplanting easy and safe.

Pruning is best done in late winter or spring, at a time when the trees are leafless. Branches need to be thinned occasionally to prevent overcrowding.

The horse chestnut has a number of close relatives, including the red horse chestnut, the red buckeye and the sweet buckeye. For small gardens the bottle-brush buckeye, so called because of the long spikes of white flowers which resemble a bottle brush, is an excellent choice. The bottle-brush buckeye grows only 7 to 10 feet high. It is native to the southeastern United States but is also hardy farther north. It spreads by means of sucker growths from the ground and may be easily increased by detaching one of these and planting it in March.

CHINABERRY (Melia azedarach)

This tree, sometimes called soapberry or Indian soap plant, grows on moist clay soils or dry limestone uplands. It ranges through Oklahoma, New Mexico and Arizona, becoming a tree 40 to 50 feet tall and 1 to 2 feet in diameter. It has erect branches and many-angled branchlets. The bark is broken by deep fissures into long narrow plates which, in turn, are broken on the surface into small red-brown scales. The leaves, appearing in March or April, bear 4 to 9 pairs of alternate lance-shaped leaflets which are pale yellow-green.

CHINABERRY

The whitish flowers are displayed in large, dense clusters. The fruit, ripening in September and October, does not fall until spring. It is yellow, clustered on short branchlets, and has dark brown seeds.

Chinaberries will thrive in mild climates if planted in a sunny position. They prefer a deep, sandy loam and must be kept moist at the roots during the summer.

Propagation may be accomplished with cuttings, which consist of well-ripened side shoots. They should be detached with a "heel" of the old wood and inserted in a greenhouse in July or August.

DATE, CHINESE (Zizyphus)

The most important tree in this group is the common jujube, or Chinese date, as it is frequently called. This is a small, thorny tree which makes a very handsome appearance because of its deep green, glossy leaves which seem to fairly shine and sparkle in the sun.

The jujube is one tree that never fails to bear fruit. The blossoms, small, greenish and insignificant, do not appear on the tree until late in spring, well after the last frost. They are followed by a green fruit, usually elongated in appearance, which resembles a date. This resemblance becomes even greater in the late summer or fall as the fruit turns brownish and drops from the tree. The fruits are used dried and may also be preserved in syrup.

The jujube will thrive on poor ground, but will do better if given more favorable conditions. It likes an alkaline soil and is a good tree for the Southwest.

Jujubes should be planted 20 to 25 feet apart. Propagation is by root cuttings and by grafting superior varieties on understocks raised from seeds.

Jujubes may be leaf-losing or evergreen, depending on the part of the country they are grown in. They are found wild in Texas, California and Mexico and have naturalized in many sections.

ELM (Ulmus)

Do you remember a favorite elm tree from your childhood? Did you play for long happy hours under the welcome shade of its spreading branches? The American elm is a very familiar tree to most of us, for it grows everywhere east of the Rocky Mountains. It is a hardy and cheerful tree and, deservedly, has been frequently planted both as a street tree and as a single, handsome specimen.

The elm is a wide spreading tree, almost always growing naturally into a symmetrical vase shape with slender limbs and drooping twigs. Its trunk has furrowed, light gray bark with paler branches and reddish-brown twigs.

The flowers are small and greenish. They appear before the leaves in very early spring.

The fruit is a light green, oval, winged fruit with the seed portion in the center. A deep notch in the end of the wing is characteristic of the species. The seed ripens in the spring and is widely distributed by the wind.

The elm is the famous shade tree of New England whose range extends southward even to Texas. Within this vast area, it is quite common, except in the high mountains and wet bottomlands. It reaches an average height of 60 to 70 feet and a diameter of 2 to 3 feet. The main disadvantage is its susceptibility to Dutch elm disease.

The slippery elm is also known as the red elm and the moose elm because the wood of this elm is red and moose show great fondness for its young shoots. Children, too, find pleasure in this tree, for under the bark of young shoots a sweet substance is found, giving the tree its common name. To get at this, the bark is stripped and its inner surface scraped.

Slippery elm also has medicinal properties, and poultices are made of the bark to relieve throat and chest ailments. It is also thought to alleviate fevers and inflammatory disorders. The inner bark is sometimes dried and ground. When mixed with milk, it becomes a valuable food for invalids.

The rock elm, another relative, chooses dry, gravelly uplands or low, heavy clay soil in which to grow. Its leaves are small, firm and dark green. Sometimes called the cork elm, this refers to the corky bark which runs out in winged ridges, even on the twigs.

The winged elm is a small and dainty member of the family, but it is a pretty round-headed little tree suitable for planting in small yards. Even the seeds of this tree are long and slender.

The English elm is a favorite for planting in parks in our eastern states. Less graceful than our American species, it is characterized by a stockier look. However, its leaves hang

ELM

on longer in the autumn, remaining pretty and green long after those on the American elms have dropped and blown away.

The Scotch elm is still another which should be better known. Before the leaves open, this tree often looks bright green when seen from a distance. This is caused by the winged seeds, which are very large and numerous, crowding the twigs and giving the tree an exceptionally interesting appearance.

FIG (Ficus carica)

This gentleman is best known for the edible fruits produced by the common fig, Ficus carica, which is a native of the Mediterranean region. Figs may be grown either as trees or in a bushy, shrubby form with many shoots. The tree form is, of course, the most practical for shade. To achieve this the young tree should be trained to one central trunk. Work also, as you prune, for well-spaced branches that are mechanically strong and not likely to be broken or damaged by high winds or storms. In addition, you should try to encourage the development of strong, healthy branches that will bear a crop of good figs, possibly even during the first season.

This crop, which is borne on the shoots of the current season's branches, may actually be the second crop that the fig will bear, as a crop is usually borne on the older shoots that have lived through the winter. As the tree grows older and becomes established you may expect at least 2 crops each year. In warm countries, a third crop may be borne in late summer or early fall.

Figs are easy to grow. The soil should be moist and fertile, but with the addition of compost, they may be grown on almost any soil. Plant your tree in either winter or spring and take great care to make sure the roots do not dry out. Set the tree 2 to 4 inches deeper than it stood in the nursery row, spread the roots out carefully and pack good soil between them firmly. Water at once and see that the tree is kept moist during the first growing season. After planting, the tree should be cut back to a height of about 2 feet.

GINGKO

The gingko is a familiar tree in our big city parks and streets. It grows well in spite of polluted air, dry conditions prevalent in most cities, salt used to melt ice on sidewalks and other problems encountered in the city.

GINGKO

SWEET GUM

The gingko is sometimes called the maidenhair tree because its odd, fan-shaped leaves resemble the fronds of the maidenhair fern. Pollen of the gingko tree is like the swimming spores of ferns and instead of being carried by winds or insects, it must swim to the female flowers through dew or rain.

The gingko is a beautiful, hardy tree and in the Orient will grow 90 to 100 feet tall, sometimes attaining a girth of 18 to 20 feet. The leaves, which are bright green in summer, change to gold in the fall. Male and female flowers are borne on different trees. The fruits resemble small yellow plums. They are about ½ to ¾ inch in diameter and have a large central seed enclosed in the pulp.

GUM, SOUR (Nyssa)

The black gum, often called sour gum, of the South ranges widely, being hardy in even southern Ontario and Maine. This tree is distinguished by its tall, slender trunk, which is clothed with short, ridged, horizontal branches. It has little claim to symmetry, yet it is striking and picturesque seen against the winter sky.

More attractive in summer, it is then covered with dark, polished leaves, 2 to 4 inches long. In autumn, patches of red appear on the leaves as they begin to drop, their signal of the approach of winter. Soon the tree becomes a pillar of flame. Many people like to cut sprays of the leaves and bring them in the house for decoration. The leathery leaves do not curl and dry in the warm air of the house. The bark on younger trees is furrowed between flat ridges.

The fruit is a dark blue drupe, ⅓ to ⅔ of an inch long, containing a single hard-shelled seed. It is borne on long stems, 2 to 3 in a cluster.

Black gums will grow in many types of soil and conditions of soil moisture.

GUM, SWEET (Liquidambar styraciflua)

The sweet gum is known by the various names of blackgum, sourgum, pepperridge and tupelo. It is a handsome tree commonly found along moist roadsides and in the woods. Two southeastern species of tupelo grow in swamps, and one of these has large red fruit from which preserves are made. Tupelo honey has a distinct and delicious flavor, and when the trees are in blossom they are literally alive with bees seeking the sweet nectar.

The sweet gum is a tall tree with a straight trunk, about 4 or 5 feet in diameter and its slender branches are covered with ridged corky bark. Many people consider this very ornamental.

The head of the sweet gum is at first regular and pyramidal, but as the tree grows older, it becomes irregularly oblong and somewhat narrow. The older bark is reddish-brown in color and becomes deeply furrowed.

The star-shaped leaves have 5 to 7 points, or lobes, and are also 5 to 7 inches across. They are very aromatic. In the fall the coloring is brilliant, ranging from pale yellow through orange and red to a deep bronze. As they flame through these variations of color, the trees are among the most handsome in the forest.

The fruit at first glance reminds one of the balls of the sycamores, but on closer inspection proves to be a head. It measures an inch or more in diameter and is made up of many capsules with projecting spines. It frequently hangs on the tree by its long, swinging stem late into the winter. Sweet gum balls are often sprayed with metallics and used in bouquets for winter decorations.

HACKBERRY (Celtis)

Hackberries are among our hardiest and most widely distributed shade trees. Though they will grow in almost any soil or location, they reach their handsome best in moist soil along stream borders or in marshes where they may reach a height of 125 feet or more.

The southern hackberry, sometimes called the sugarberry, is a medium-sized tree seldom growing taller than 50 feet. It may be from 10 to 20 inches in diameter, though occasionally larger. Its limbs form a broad head, and its branchlets are slender and light green,

sometimes covered with fine soft hairs when young. During their first winter, the twigs are a bright reddish-brown. In the open, the hackberry makes a very symmetrical crown, an excellent quality for a shade tree.

The bark is pale gray and lumpy. The leaves are lance-shaped and 2½ to 5 inches long.

The inconspicuous flowers appear in April

HACKBERRY

or May and are of a creamy-green color. The small berries are orange red or yellow, deepening in color as they mature.

It is the sweet taste of the berries which gives rise to the name sugarberry. The berries are a favorite food of birds and animals. In a way, this is the tree's only fault, for the dropping of the seeds can be a great nuisance in the fall of the year. In the South, hackberries are often used to line sidewalks and the berries pop like tiny firecrackers when they are stepped upon.

HONEY LOCUST, THORNLESS
(Gleditsia triacanthos inermis)

As a shade tree for lawn or avenue, the honey locust has long been a great favorite. It is a tall, handsome, flat-topped tree growing 125 feet tall under favorable conditions.

The bell-shaped flowers appear in elongated clusters. They are followed by long, bean-like pods which usually remain on the trees during the winter. The leaves are almost full-grown when the blossoms appear and it is their feathery, fern-like aspect which is the trees' greatest charm.

Honey locusts thrive best in an open sunny location and in deep, well-drained, but moist, loamy soil. Plant them in either fall or spring.

Little pruning is ever necessary for a honey locust, as the tree is naturally well-shaped. Pruning consists of shortening an occasional too-long branch which may spoil the symmetry of the tree. When the trees are young, a straight leading shoot should be carefully maintained to form the trunk.

Honey locusts may be propagated by seeds sown in sandy soil, but it takes a lot of soaking to prepare the hard seeds for sprouting. To hasten the process, the seeds are sometimes scalded. In nature they are soaked by the rains, frozen during the winter and thawed by the warm air of spring.

There are several varieties of honey locust, the best of which is the thornless one for obvious reasons.

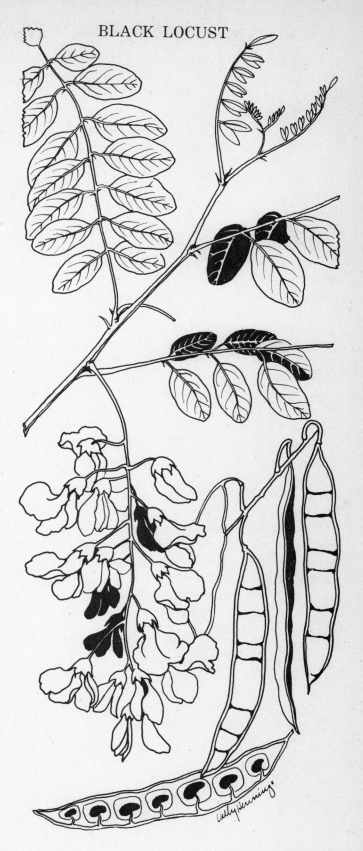

BLACK LOCUST

HORNBEAM (Carpinus)

The hornbeams are delightful little trees, both interesting and unusual. Long ago they earned the name of "ironwood" because their wood is heavy, close-grained and extremely hard. Once they were used in the construction of levers, mallets and for the beams of ox yokes. Ironwood outwears the toughest elm and the stoutest oak, yet the wood is springy enough to use for fork handles. Bowls and dishes made from the wood never leak or crack.

The American hornbeam has blue-gray bark of fine texture, and from this it is commonly called the "blue beech." In others the name "water beech" shows the tree's liking for rich swampy land.

In favorable environments the hornbeams form symmetrical oval heads, and their branches are finely divided into many wiry, supple twigs. The slender tree is seldom over 20 to 30 feet high and 7 to 10 inches in diameter.

The 2- to 3-inch-long leaves are pointed and doubly toothed along the margin.

KATSURA TREE
(Cercidiphyllum japonicum)

The katsura tree is a hardy, leaf-losing, ornamental tree of pyramidal growth. The attractive leaves are violet-tinted when young, then become a pale green in summer and golden in the autumn. The leaves resemble those of the redbud tree, to which the katsura is related.

Two kinds of katsura are known, and both are found growing wild in eastern Asia. The best known of these, Cercidiphyllum japonicum, is also unusual in that it generally has several trunks. It will sometimes reach a height of 90 to 100 feet. This species has heart-shaped leaves. The blossoms are unattractive. They are followed, when fertilized, by pod-like fruits. The Chinese tree, Cercidiphyllum japonicum sinense, grows with a straight trunk. A somewhat more attractive tree in shape, it is less hardy.

Katsuras thrive in well-drained loamy soil, and planting may be done in fall or spring. They need little pruning other than to prevent overcrowding of the branches and to keep the tree's shape symmetrical. It should be done during the winter.

Katsuras are easily propagated by layering or from seeds, which should be planted in autumn.

LINDEN (Tilia)

The lindens, or basswoods, are a family of tropical trees with about thirty-five genera. Their many good qualities include swift growth, excellent framework, clean, smooth bark and beautiful, fragrant blossom. And the flowers are followed by masses of seed clusters, gracefully winged, which in turn decorate the foliage. Possibly the only fault of the linden is its early dropping of its leaves. This occurs especially in windy sections, and the winds also mar the appearance of the leaves soon after they reach maturity.

The veined leaves are large and heart-shaped. The flowers yield an excellent honey. The tree grows to a height of 60 to 100 feet in a favorable environment. The wood is light and fine-grained and is used in woodenware, cabinetwork and for toys.

The range of the American species extends from New Brunswick to the Dakotas and south to Virginia and Texas.

LOCUST (Acacia)

The acacias, or wattles as they are sometimes called, are native to Australia. Liking a warm climate, they are frequently grown in California and other warm areas.

Acacias are trees of great variety and beauty both in flower and evergreen foliage. They are widely planted as street trees and specimen trees for the home landscape.

The leaves are set on a branching stem. The tiny leaflets give the tree an exceptionally graceful, feathery appearance. Their lacy, fern-like foliage would justify their planting, but there is much more that the tree has to offer.

The flowers bloom in a profuse mass, almost

LINDEN

obscuring the tree with a veil of white or gold. The individual flowers, which may be white or yellow, are each very small but they crowd so abundantly on the button-like heads or elongated spikes that they almost overwhelm the tree.

In their native Australia, the acacias flower even more abundantly than in this country. But after flowering, this little tree has still not stopped "giving," for in most species there are still the interesting curling pods which pass through many color changes before they finally discharge their seeds.

Though Australia has the largest number of species of acacias, there are others which grow wild in Africa, Asia, tropical and temperate South America, the West Indies, Central America, Mexico and the southwestern region of the United States. Acacias can even be grown in southern England where they often attain good size and are called "tassel trees."

MAGNOLIA

Frequently planted throughout the South as street trees, or specimens for the home lawn, the magnificent magnolias are difficult to surpass. With its straight trunk, large symmetrical head made up of large, shining green leaves and its gorgeous fragrant flowers, the southern magnolia is almost unbelievably beautiful. This handsome tree prefers the rich, moist soil of swamps and riverbanks where it attains its fullest glory, but it is adaptable under cultivation. I have even seen excellent specimens growing in very dry locations.

Unfortunately magnolias are not hardy enough for planting in the North, but they are grown extensively in all sections where the climate is to their liking. The tree's natural range is from the North Carolina coast to Tampa Bay and west along the Gulf Coast to Texas and southern Arkansas. It is also widely grown in California as a street tree, especially in the southern part where it ornaments many parks and gardens.

The flowers, which look like great roses,

are distinctly visible from a long distance, their whiteness shining like beacon lights. They are set off to perfection by the lustrous, dark green foliage. The flowers are intensely fragrant; some think it is overpowering, especially if the flowers are cut and brought indoors. It is, however, most enticing to bees and other insects.

The great laurel magnolia may lift its head 50 to 80 feet above the ground and possesses a trunk 4 feet thick. Each leaf cluster will hold one of the great, waxy-white flowers, some of which are 7 to 8 inches across.

MAPLES (Acer)

Acer, a single genus, includes 60 to 70 species which are widely distributed over the Northern Hemisphere. Surprisingly, one species goes south of the equator to the mountains of Java.

All maples produce pale, close-grained, moderately hard wood, valued for furniture and the interiors of houses. Perhaps, best of all, the clear sap of certain American species is made into that delectable confection known as maple sugar.

How can you tell when a maple is a maple? There are two ways to do this; they have opposite, simple leaves, palm-shaped, veined and lobed, and they have typical paired, winged fruits. The maples' habits remain completely unchanged under cultivation and no other tree has both leaves and fruits like the maples.

MAPLE, SUGAR

This member of the maple family needs no introduction for everyone knows about its sugary sap, highly favored for the making of maple sugar and maple syrup. It is a glorious sight in autumn, brightening the October landscape as its leaves turn from yellow to orange and finally to brilliant red. These leaves are firm and broad, cleft shallowly into five lobes and are often toothed as well.

The flowers of this species of maple open rather late and hang in hairy clusters on the new shoots. The fruits are smooth, plump and winged.

SUGAR MAPLE

Valuable as this maple is for lumber, it is still more so as a shade tree, for it is slow growing, resists damage by storms and has no messy habits.

MAPLE, RED

This member of the family likes moisture and loves to live in swamps. It will, however, even thrive on a hillside provided it has plenty of moisture. It is often planted in parks and along city streets.

This is the most beautiful of all the maples. In early spring its swelling buds glow like garnet among the brown twigs. The newly opened flowers have red petals; even the first leaves that accompany the blooms are red.

In May, the dainty flat seedpods become cockscomb red, exquisitely beautiful against the bright green of the young foliage. Again in early September the tree becomes a splash of scarlet. The red maple never forgets its name, not even in winter, for then the knotty twigs gleam red against the gray trunk.

MESQUITE, HONEY (Propis glandulosa)

The shade of the honey mesquite is thin, yet it may be the most important shade tree of all to those who live in or near the arid regions of the Southwest. The wide branches may cast their shadows across as much as 50 feet and the sand below is covered by pods which animals seek avidly.

Mesquite grows from Texas to southern California, has thorny branches, feathery gray leaves, masses of golden flowers and honey-sweet pods. A true desert dweller, the mesquite is an indicator of water and its root system may extend downward to a depth of 30 or 40 feet with many radiating roots. In fact a large part of the mesquite tree lives below the ground, and the often smallish tree or bush seen above represents only a small part of the wood of the tree.

The leaves are compound with two and sometimes four leaflets arranged on each side of a common stem. Mesquite flowers are tiny and borne in clusters or spikes from 2 to 4 inches long.

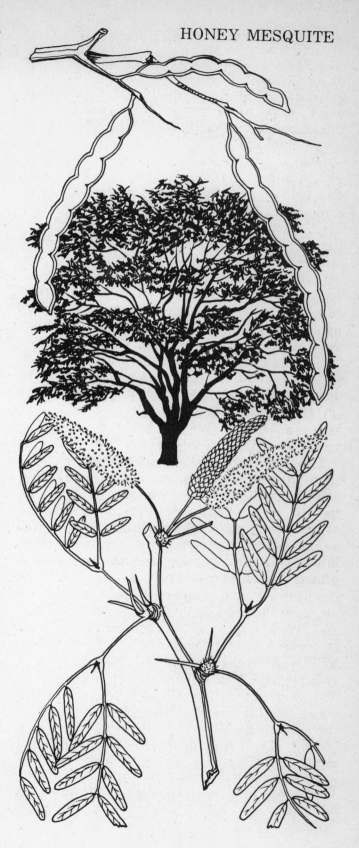

HONEY MESQUITE

MIMOSA (Albizia julibrissin)

Mimosa trees are absolutely exquisite when in bloom, the small heads resembling pink powderpuffs. It is a small tree, reaching a height of 30 to 40 feet at the most, and for this reason is especially suited to a small landscape planting.

In the North, mimosas are sometimes grown as potted plants in greenhouses. They should be potted in March, preferably in a compost of loam and leaf mold with a little sand. The addition of peat is also beneficial. Plants should be progressively repotted into larger receptacles as they grow. They are usually placed outdoors in May or early in June, after being hardened off in a cold frame. In severe climates they will freeze during the winter and are not recommended for growing outdoors.

When pruning becomes necessary, either outdoors or in the greenhouse, it should be done in early spring.

MULBERRY, PAPER
(Broussonetia papyrifera)

These may be either tall shrubs or small trees, depending on the manner in which they are trained. They are especially valuable for their very strong-growing stems and large, ornamental leaves which fall in the autumn.

The best known of the paper mulberries is hardy even in northern sections and is often planted as a street tree. It will grow to medium height, approximately 30 feet or more. Male and female flowers are produced on separate trees. The male flowers, borne in woolly, yellowish catkins, are 2 to 3 inches long while those on the female trees are in small, round heads about ½-inch in diameter. The flowers open in the spring and, if fertilized, are followed by red fruits.

Paper mulberries do well in any ordinary garden soil if it is deeply dug and enriched with well-composted manure. They may be planted in either spring or fall.

Pruning is seldom necessary for the tree has a naturally fine shape. Cut out only weak or crowded twigs and shorten any long branches which may spoil the symmetrical shape of the tree. Cutting back should be done in the fall or winter months.

Paper mulberries are easily increased by cuttings taken during August and September. These cuttings, 6 to 10 inches long, are taken from side shoots. A thin "heel" should also be detached. Place them in a bed of light, sandy soil in a cold frame.

MULBERRY

MULBERRY, WHITE (Morus alba)

The mulberry family is a large one indeed, including nearly a thousand species of tropical and temperate-zone plants. Mulberries are not grown commercially, as the fruit is considered too soft and insipid for marketing, but a tree or two in a large garden or on a farm are considered worthwhile.

The fruit ripens over a long period of time and is beloved by birds and useful for feeding poultry and pigs, as well as being liked by some people for eating out of hand. The fruits may be white, red or black. In form they resemble blackberries. As a lawn tree the mulberry is nicely formed for shade but the dropping of the berries makes it somewhat messy. Some types which do not drop fruit are now available.

OAK (Quercus)

The oaks have one very definite characteristic in common—acorns!

As soon as they come to fruiting age, all oak trees bear acorns and this, the world over, is the sign by which the oaks are known. You can recognize a full-grown tree almost immediately for the little cups often cling to the branches after the nuts have fallen.

Though all oak trees bear acorns, they show remarkable differences in their cups. Some have stalked, others stalkless cups. In some the cup encloses only the base of the acorn, in others the tip of the acorn is barely exposed. Others have cups roughened by large irregular scales; in still others the cups are smooth. Some types mature their acorns 6 months after blossoming, but 18 months may elapse between flowering and the acorns in other types.

There are many types of oak trees, some preferring a moist environment, others willing to grow on almost any soil or in any location, sunny or shady.

The white oak is especially valuable as a lumber tree. The burr oak is so called because of its mossy cups with loose, fringed scales. The post oak has wood noted for its durability when in contact with the soil and has been

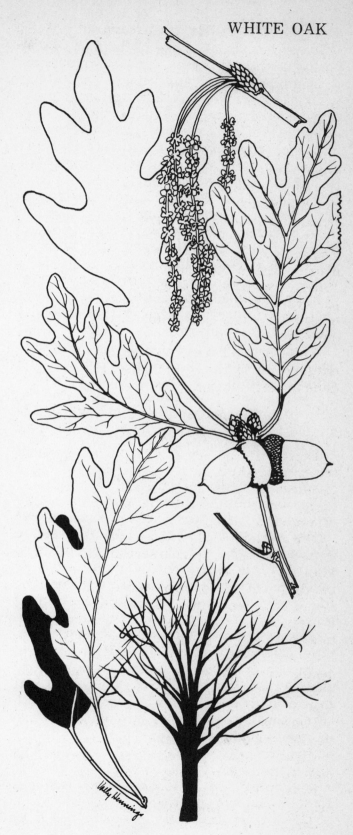

widely used for posts by farmers.

The chestnut oak is one of the most desirable for planting in parks, for it is symmetrical with handsome bark and foliage. The swamp white oak loves to stand in wet ground, sometimes even growing in actual swamps.

The basket oak has wood that splits readily into thin, tough plates. Bushel baskets, china crates and other types of woven wares are made from the oak splints.

The live oak is widely planted in southern cities such as New Orleans. This is the oak most commonly seen displaying a drapery of Spanish moss, looking ghostly at twilight or across the edge of a low-lying swamp. Many think this moss is a parasite but it is not. It is a plant which draws its sustenance from the air and is merely a lodger on the oak whose vitality it does not sap.

Other oak trees are the black oak; scarlet oak, so named because of its flaming autumn colors; the pin oak whose short, spur-like twigs cluster on the branches; and the red oak. Still other oaks are the willow oak, whose supple twigs bend willow-like; the single or laurel oak and the mountain live oak.

PECAN (Carya)

The best nuts in the whole hickory family are borne by the pecan, and it is considered one of the most profitable orchard trees in sections where it can be grown. Pecans have a lot going for them. Not only are the nuts tasty, nutritious and abundantly borne, but the tree itself is one of our loveliest shade trees.

The pecan is the largest of the hickories, often attaining a height of 100 feet or more. It forms a large, rounded top of symmetrical shape. The outer bark is rough and hard, but broken into scales. On the limbs it is smooth when the tree is young, but tends to scale or divide as the tree grows older.

The leaves are similar to those of other hickories and also the black walnut. They are made up of 9 to 17 leaflets, each oblong, toothed and long-pointed.

The flowers appear in early spring and hang in interesting tassels from 2 to 3 inches long. The nuts have a husk which divides along its grooved seams when it ripens in the fall. The nuts vary in size and in thickness of the shell, but have been greatly improved in cultivated varieties.

Pecans are somewhat difficult to transplant because of the long tap root. They grow readily from seed and it is often advisable to grow them in this way. Plant the seed where the trees are to grow and then have them grafted to named nut varieties when they are of sufficient size. This is so easily done that anyone with even a slight knowledge of grafting can accomplish it. I have three pecan trees growing in my yard right now which I grafted myself many years ago.

PISTACIA, CHINESE (Pistacia chinensis)

These natives of the Mediterranean region and China are shrubs or small trees. Many are of considerable decorative and economic importance in subtropical areas, but will not live outdoors in northern countries.

The nuts which follow the rather insignificant flowers are of value in some species and are sometimes called "green almonds." Pistacia trees are grown for these nuts and for their decorative value in California and the southern United States.

The nut has a thin, hard shell opening at the edge much like the shell of an oyster. This husk is removed before the kernel is processed. The kernel may be ground and used as a food flavoring and is particularly delicious in ice cream and candy. The texture of the kernel is very fine and the flavor delicate. The kernels can also be salted in brine while still in the shell.

The pistacia tree grows well in dry regions. Seldom rising to a height of more than 30 feet, its branches spread widely. The leaves are thick and resinous and drop off during the winter.

Every pistacia tree is either male or female. To produce nuts the female trees must have a male tree growing nearby to produce pollen for their flowers.

PLANE TREE, ORIENTAL (Platanus)

This member of the sycamore family is a favorite for planting as a street tree and is a good choice for a lawn tree. About one-third of the street trees of Paris are plane trees. This tree is particularly noteworthy because it is unusually hardy, forms a symmetrical, compact pyramid in shape and is also free from injury by smoke and dust.

The plane tree also has the advantage of rapid growth, even in the poor soil which is often all that is available along city streets.

The Oriental plane tree dangles more than one round ball from each stem but is still easily recognizable as a sycamore because of its bark-shedding habit. It is far less subject to the ravages of insects and fungi than our native species.

POPLARS (Populus)

The poplars are a large and rather commonplace family of trees. They are well adapted for shelter belts and will endure severe pruning.

In the dry plains of the middle west, the cottonwoods, or poplars, make valuable shade trees, but for this purpose only male trees should be planted. The reason for this is the great amount of cottony material shed by the females when they produce seeds. This fills the air, littering lawns and gardens almost like a fall of snow.

Though poplars do well in dry countries, some of them are excellent trees for planting in moist places, either in small groups or as specimen trees. One, the Carolina poplar, makes an admirable street tree.

If you would plant a poplar, however, consider the fact that their large root systems will travel great distances in search of moisture and may interfere with other trees and shrubs and occasionally clog drains and sewers. Another fault is the brittleness of their branches which are very subject to storm and wind damage. Sometimes large branches break off when this happens, spoiling the shape of the tree.

Poplar trees grow quickly—and abundantly due to their tremendous production of seed. And the wind sows it far and wide. Young poplar trees love the sun, and often serve as nurse trees to more valuable hardwoods and conifers which need shade to become successfully established. By the time the young trees of other species are able to take care of themselves the poplars have quite likely matured and disappeared for their life span is short.

Poplars are, however, very tenacious of life. The roots often send up suckers from beneath the ground. Cutting these off only encourages them to grow more vigorously.

POPLAR

POPLAR, TULIP (Liriodendron tulipifera)

This is a stately tree which may reach a height of 200 feet with a trunk 10 feet in diameter when grown under favorable forest conditions. Under cultivation it is much smaller but still impressive at maturity. It is also a valuable lumber tree. At no time of the year is the tulip tree without interest or beauty. Even in the dead of winter its symmetrical shape is attractive. The squarish leaves are peculiarly notched and quite broad, making identification easy. The tree is named for the greenish-yellow, tulip-like flowers which open in May and June. The buds, closed by two purse-like scales, are unique.

TULIP TREE

SASSAFRAS

The aromatic sassafras tree is the sole remnant of an ancient genus. It is a beautiful tree that brightens the fall woods.

Deep in the woodland it may reach a height of 100 feet or more, and it is an important lumber tree. Long ago, the Indians told the colonists in Florida about the curative qualities of the sassafras tree, and its reputation traveled far and wide. People still make and drink a tea from sassafras bark "to clear the blood." In the Southwest, the leaves are also used as an ingredient in soups called "gumbo file" and "gombo zab." In New England the bark was used to make an orange dye. It is also called the "ague tree" because the tea made of the bark was once used as a stimulant for warming the body of those who suffered from malarial "ague" or "chills and fever."

But aside from all the uses and legends surrounding the sassafras tree, it is still most useful as a shade tree on the home grounds. In winter it is picturesque because of the angular twist of its stout, short branches. In the spring, the bare twigs are made lovely by the delicate green of the new leaves. It again draws admiration when its blue berries on their scarlet pedicels appear.

SERVICEBERRY (Amelanchier)

The serviceberry, also known as the service tree and sometimes as "sarvis," is one of the hardiest and most beautiful of our spring-flowering trees. It is a small tree, suitable for home planting, and will grow 20 to 50 feet tall with a rather narrow, rounded top. The bark is thin and ashy gray.

The leaves are slender-stalked, rounded and finely toothed. They are 2 to 4 inches long and purplish-brown in color until nearly mature when they become a light green.

The white flowers appear in clusters in early spring, making the tree very conspicuous. The fruit is rounded, and, when ripe, dark purple. It is ½-inch in diameter and ripens in May or June. Birds and other forest creatures are very fond of the fruit.

All of the amelanchiers, some of which are known as Juneberries or shadbushes, will thrive in any good garden soil but need a sunny or lightly shaded location. Though they may be planted in spring, fall is considered the best time for planting. Little pruning is ever necessary.

The reddish-purple fruits of the amelanchiers were a source of food for various American Indian tribes and are sometimes used to make jellies.

SYCAMORES (Platanus)

In Europe the sycamore is called the plane tree. It is considered the largest hardwood tree in our forests and reaches its fullest potential along streams and on rich bottom-lands. It is one of the fastest-growing trees.

The bark of the sycamore is its most characteristic feature. On the trunk and large limbs it is very smooth and greenish-gray in color. The outer bark flakes off each year in large patches and exposes the nearly white younger bark. Near the base of old trees the bark becomes thick, dark brown and divided in deep furrows.

The leaves are 6 to 7 inches long and almost as broad, light green and smooth. The fruit is a ball about 1 inch in diameter, conspicuous throughout the winter. During early spring the fruit ball breaks up, and the small seeds are scattered widely by the wind.

TREE OF HEAVEN (Ailanthus altissima)

This native of India and China received its name because of its height, which may be more than 100 feet when it is fully grown. It is also hardy and has large feathery leaves 12 to 20 inches long and 6 to 12 inches wide.

The male and female flowers are usually produced on separate trees, but are very insignificant. The female flowers are followed by clusters of reddish-brown winged fruits or "keys" which are attractive in autumn. Male trees give off an unpleasant odor while in flower and should never be planted.

The female tree of heaven is very valuable for planting in parks, along avenues, or on larger home grounds. It is resistant to smoke and air pollution and is also remarkably free from pests and diseases. It has even been known to live through an occasional inundation of sea water.

Pruning should be done during the winter. Remove any crowded branches and keep the leading shoot clear of other shoots or branches.

If the ground beneath a tree of heaven is forked over, suckers may develop from any damaged or broken roots. These can be easily and safely transplanted.

WALNUT (Juglans)

The black walnut is a handsome, stately tree of great dignity and beauty. It is a tree of open woods and roadsides. It is also a beautiful shade tree for the home grounds and will add much elegance to any landscape.

The large, fragrant leaves have 15 or more small leaflets, each finely toothed and ending in a long point. They are smooth above and hairy below.

The walnut bears conspicuous catkins of male flowers and very insignificant female flowers that are succeeded by delicious nuts. The black walnut is a nut to be savored. One should eat only a very few at a time as they are very rich in oil. The husks which cover the nuts turn from green to yellow to brown. Once the husk is off, the nuts must be cracked carefully. Their very thick shells make it hard to avoid breaking the meats.

In the deep forests walnuts may attain a height of 100 feet or more, but seldom grow this tall in cultivation. In open-grown trees, the stem is rather short and the crown broad and spreading.

Walnut trees grow best in well-drained loamy soil but may be grown with fair success on light land. Plant the tree where it is to grow and allow plenty of room for development. Prune the tree while young to a single leading shoot. Pruning should always be done between June and December, for if the trees are pruned during late winter or early spring they will "bleed" profusely.

WILLOW, WEEPING (Salix)

Few trees are as graceful as the weeping willow, salix babylonica. It is much planted as an ornamental tree, may grow to great size, and gives a fair amount of rather open shade.

Just what is a "weeping" tree? It is one whose twigs are soft and flexible. Instead of thrusting out stiffly from the branches, they are pendulous and dangling. Some, as in the willow, even sweep the ground. This characteristic is considered so charming that it has even been bred into many horticultural varieties of other trees. Yet for all this weepiness, the foliage of the tree has wonderful lightness and cheerfulness of expression. A willow will add much charm to the garden where it is planted.

Willows take root from twig cuttings, and thus weeping willows have become naturalized all over the world in moist ground and near streams and ponds, for this willow loves moisture and must have it.

There is much controversy over the native home of the willow, but most believe it to be China. The weeping willow is the willow of the Bible, the one that is said to have grown by the waters of Babylon.

Weeping willows are tolerant of smoke and grime and are widely cultivated in cities. The narrow, lance-shaped leaves are similar to those of other willows and are 3 to 6 inches long. The tiny seeds are covered with white hairs. The bark is grayish brown and fissured.

WEEPING WILLOW

ZELKOVA

The zelkova trees are mostly natives of Asia and are distinguished from the elms to which they are distantly related by their smoother bark, which suggests that of the beech. They also bear small, nutlike seeds. Male and female flowers are present on different parts of the same branch but neither, unfortunately, is attractive.

The zelkovas are generally increased by seeds, though suckers may be used. Plant a zelkova tree in a well-drained, loamy soil. The wood is very hard, heavy and pliable, and is used in the manufacture of furniture.

Zelkova serrata, one of the better trees of this type in cultivation, is a native of Japan. It was introduced into western gardens about 1861. This species grows 100 to 120 feet tall in its native Japan but in our gardens is more likely to develop a short trunk and a widely spreading head and branches.